Doom in the Deep

Óttar Sveinsson

English translation
Anna Yates

Doom
in the Deep

Foreword by
Sir Magnus Magnusson

THE LYONS PRESS
Guilford, Connecticut
An imprint of The Globe Pequot Press

The Lyons Press is an imprint of The Globe Pequot Press.

ISBN 1-59228-466-3

10 9 8 7 6 5 4 3 2 1

Printed in the United States of America

Designed by Rúnar Gunnarsson

Library of Congress Cataloging-in-Publication Data is available on file.

Foreword

Magnus Magnusson KBE

Mention 'Iceland', and most people in Britain associate it automatically with fish—fish, and the three post-war 'Cod Wars' between Britain and Iceland as Iceland unilaterally extended her fishing-limits: to 12 miles in 1958, to 50 miles in 1972, and to 200 miles in 1975. On each occasion, Britain sent naval frigates to the Icelandic fishing grounds to protect and shepherd the trawler fleets of Hull and Grimsby against the Icelandic coastguard vessels which tried to arrest them; and on each occasion, Britain had to give better to the Icelanders. The last Cod War ended in a final victory for the Icelanders in 1976—but Britain had the consolation, as the British Foreign Secretary wryly conceded at the time, of 'coming second'!

Mercifully, 'war' was a typically journalistic misnomer for the activities which went on around the coasts of Iceland. They were brawls rather than battles—scuffles rather than skirmishes. There were no human casualties, thank goodness. A few boats had their prows dented from collisions. A few British trawlers had their trawls sheered off with giant clippers. But the weapons were mainly words, the missiles seldom more destructive than wet haddocks. The world's media had a field-day dramatising the deeds of derring-do of individual trawler skippers and Icelandic gunboat captains (I should know, because I covered the events of the first Cod War myself in the late 1950s for the *Daily Express*!).

It all ended peacefully—which was just as well, because fishermen on the high seas have a common enemy to contend with which can be far more lethal than any Cod War could ever be: the sea itself.

From time immemorial, the sea has taken a grimly relentless toll of human life. In the years between 1948 and 1964, no fewer than 757 British seamen perished at sea. Iceland, too, has suffered terrible losses. In March 1685, in the days when fishermen went to sea in open rowing boats to pursue their perilous calling, nearly 200 men perished around the south-east coast when fierce southerly storms blew up with sudden and unpredictable fury; half of them died on a single day, March 9. On March 8, 1700, some 165 men (0.33%

of Iceland's entire population) died in the widow-making seas to the north and east, when dozens of small fishing boats were overwhelmed by a storm of unprecedented fury.

But modern times have had storms which were just as ferocious, leading to disasters which were just as spectacular, despite the much greater sophistication of modern fishing technology. The freak storm which struck the north-west coast of Iceland in the midwinter of 1968 produced the worst weather conditions there in living memory: a roaring northerly blizzard of snow combined with 10 degrees of frost. In all, 25 seamen and three vessels were lost.

Doom in the Deep is the story of that death-dealing storm and the almost incredible feats of human courage and endurance which accompanied it. On a terrible February night, a score of British and Icelandic fishing vessels battled through mountainous seas for the traditional safety of Isafjord Bay, in the West Fjords, with ice forming remorselessly on their superstructures and threatening to overturn them. The Hull trawler *Ross Cleveland* turned turtle and went down within minutes, apparently with the loss of all hands. The Icelandic motorboat *Heidrun II* disappeared. The Grimsby trawler *Notts County* ran aground in the blind darkness, and its crew had a nightmare wait while the Icelandic coastguard vessel, the *Odin*, risked everything in a daring rescue mission at huge peril to itself. All the Cod War animosities between Britain and Iceland were forgotten as men battled with exemplary courage and seamanship to save one another's lives.

In this book, Icelandic journalist Óttar Sveinsson, best-selling author of several books on sea-rescues and true-life struggles with the elements, vividly retells the story of the Great Storm through the eyes and words of many of the survivors and eye-witnesses—particularly Richard Moore of the *Notts County*, who now lives in Clydebank, near Glasgow, and Harry Eddom, the First Mate and only survivor of the *Ross Cleveland*, who escaped death in a horrendous ordeal before being found. Also featured are Sigurdur Arnason, the skipper of the *Odin*, and his gallant crew, who dared all in tiny inflatable rafts in those deadly conditions to rescue 18 men off the stranded *Notts County*.

It is a story of incomparable courage and heroism, of disaster and despair: an unforgettable tribute to the spirit and hardihood of the brave men who go down to the sea in ships—and sometimes go down with them. The tale is nobly served by the fluent translation into English by Anna Yates.

Doom in the Deep

Doom in the Deep

A small man in an overcoat, with a cigarette hanging from the corner of his mouth, knocked at the door of a dilapidated house in Cleethorpes on the outskirts of Grimsby. Indoors was 25-year-old Richard Moore, known to his friends as Dick. Originally from the south of England, he had been living in this east-coast port for the past two years. He had been without work for about a week, and was waiting for a berth on one of the many side-trawlers that sailed from the fishing ports on the Humber: Hull on the north side, Grimsby on the south. Most of the deep-sea trawlers sailing from these ports fished off the Icelandic coast.

The thin man at Dick's door was from Consolidated Fisheries, the company that operated the trawler *Notts County*. It was the middle of winter, late January 1968. Outside the weather was cold and damp, and the murky, polluted waters of the river gave off a salty tang of the sea.

Dick was waking up. "Who can that be at this time of night?" he thought.

At the door, the trawler-company man was impatiently running his fingers through his dark, greasy hair. "Hello, is anyone there?" he called out.

"Yes, I'm coming, I'm coming," Dick called back, as he pushed the bedclothes back and got out of bed. Through the soles of his feet, he felt the damp chill of the floor in his rented room. He rubbed his hands together to try to warm them up, threw on his dressing gown and slippers, and opened the door.

"Good morning," said the man. "Are you Richard Moore?"

"Yes, that's me," Dick replied, clearing his throat and discreetly trying to rub the sleep from his eyes.

"I'm John Nagle, an agent for Consolidated. We've got the trawler *Notts County* at anchor in the river waiting to sail for Iceland, but two of the crew have failed to turn up. We had your application for a berth, and knew you were willing to go on standby. The ship sailed last night and went through the locks on the tide. If you still want to go, and are willing to join her in the river, you'll have to get a move on."

Dick was quick to respond. Unemployment was high, and when work was offered, you had to be ready to jump to it. He thought of a ship, fully crewed except for him, waiting out on the Humber. He knew the skipper would be impatiently waiting to be off. And the crew would be annoyed at hanging around at anchor. They wanted to be out at sea, working, or else home with their families or girlfriends. Or even down the pub. Not stuck at anchor, almost within shouting distance of their homes, with nothing to do but wait.

Dick realized that on this trip he wouldn't be walking up the gangway with his sea bag on his shoulder, and settling into his cabin along with the rest of the crew. Instead, he and one other man would be ferried out to the ship, no doubt to be called various unrepeatable names by some of the crew, as they clustered around the rope ladder and hung over the bulwarks, thinking that if those two had not agreed to a tide jump they might have had another night ashore in the company of their families or girlfriends, or even a night at the pub knocking back a few beers, as the ship would have had to return to the dock on the next tide. This one extra night can mean a lot to a trawlerman, as they generally only get two or three nights ashore between trips that can last up to three or four weeks. Superstitions were strong among

Dick Moore at the age of 25.

❏ Tíminn

trawlermen; and one of the worst omens of all was to board a vessel out at anchor.

A strong and energetic man, Dick imagined the sort of reception he would be given, but he needed the money. After hurriedly packing his bag, he took a final look around his room and noticed the silver-plated Parker pen that his mother had given him just before she died six years back. Instinctively he felt that he had to take the pen with him, so he snatched it up and put it in his pocket. He had to set off at once; like anyone else, he needed the work. His pay was not high enough to allow him to stay ashore for long. For a week's work, a deckhand was paid about £12 6s., and 20% of that was deducted for income tax. A pound would buy a few packets of cigarettes at that time. Although trawlermen were badly paid, their job was one of the most hazardous lines of work known in Great Britain. A trawlerman was almost three times more likely to die at work than a miner. In the period 1948 to 1964, 757 British seaman had lost their lives at sea.

Dick Moore was born in Glasgow in April 1942. His mother Josephine was of Irish extraction; and his Dutch father had been chief engineer on British freighters during World War II.

Dick had started his career at sea in the merchant marine, before becoming a trawlerman. On trawlers, he was generally employed as a deckhand, but sometimes worked in the engine room:

"I'd been on the trawler *Ross Lynx*, but I'd lost my berth the previous week when she went into dry dock. And now the *Notts County* was waiting. She was a 441-ton trawler. She'd sailed from Grimsby during the night, through the locks, to catch the high tide. I'd felt lucky at the time that the company had picked my name out when they found they were two men short, even knowing I would have to take some 'stick' when I boarded the ship. The company man went on his way, and I was sent by taxi with Frank McGuinness, the other deckhand, down to the river, where a tug was waiting. When the tug came up alongside the trawler I saw the crew of the *Notts County* gathering at the side of the ship, where a rope ladder had been let down. The comments I'd expected came flying at us.

'You can't board a ship in the middle of the river,' shouted someone. I avoided looking up. It wasn't our fault, we just needed the work. We had a living to earn.

The skipper was pleased. Now he could sail, and earn money. He was the best paid. I thought I saw a discreet smile on his face as he stood on the bridge wing, sturdy and confidence-inspiring. He obviously had a lot of experience, and I took to him at once.

The ship was fully crewed, and everything was ready. The skipper's strategy had worked. If he hadn't sailed on the evening tide, he would still be waiting in harbour for the next high tide.

'Up anchor,' the skipper shouted. The crew jumped to engage the capstan, and started hauling the anchor in."

Soon Jack Stony, the 53-year-old boatswain, called up to the captain on the bridge: "Anchor away."

The Notts County *on the Humber, headed for Grimsby Harbour.*

❏ The Grimsby Telegraph

"About bloody time," replied the skipper, and rang for "Half speed ahead" on the engine-room telegraph. The engineers brought the main engine up to half power. Black smoke billowed from the trawler's funnel. The *Notts County*, GY 643, was under way to Iceland.

Twenty-six-year-old Harry Eddom lived in Hull, at the north of the Humber. His trawler, the *Ross Cleveland*, H 61, was also bound for Iceland. The 659-ton trawler had been built in Aberdeen in 1949. There were twenty men aboard the *Ross Cleveland*, one more than the crew of the *Notts County*.

Harry Eddom's circumstances were better than Dick Moore's on the *Notts County*. He was first mate on the *Ross Cleveland*, after having attended college for three months to gain his mate's ticket. After another year at sea he would be eligible to return to college for another three months for his skipper's ticket. And that was what Harry planned to do.

Jack Stony, boatswain of the Notts County, *and one of the most experienced men aboard.*
❑ Morgunblaðið

He had always done well in his work—he was hardworking, resourceful, and got on well with the other men—he had leadership qualities. Thanks to his level-headedness, crews had worked well under his supervision. This young man, who aimed to captain a vessel in due course, had been at sea from the age of 15.

The skipper of the *Ross Cleveland* knew Harry well, and had sufficient confidence in him to allow him to pick members of the crew for this trip, and also for the last trip they had made:

"Philip Gay, the captain, knew that over the past few months I'd managed to work with a good bunch. So he'd asked me to help him pick a crew. Most of the crew of the *Ross Cleveland* had sailed with me before on my previous ship, the *Ross Illustrious*."

Harry was a happy, settled man. He had met Rita Penrose at a dance in 1963, when she was 22. He was two years older— born on July 30, 1941. He was on brief shore leave from the Hull trawler where he was a deckhand at the time. They fell in love. Harry carried on sailing on the trawlers, with short breaks in harbour to land the catch, mostly from Icelandic waters, but sometimes from the sea off Newfoundland. This meant that they

St. Andrew's Dock, Hull.

❑ Dark Winter—The Hull Daily Mail

could spend two or three days together before he was off on the next three- to four-week trip; Rita would come down to the docks to see him off, left behind like all the seamen's wives of the Humber.

After they had been going out together for a year, they announced their engagement. Rita was familiar with the life of a fisherman's family. She had grown up in the Hawthorne Avenue district of Hull, where almost everyone had some connection with the sea, fishing and trawlers. Rita's father, Arthur Penrose, had been a trawlerman, and now worked on the Liverpool-Dublin ferry. Her brother, Trevor, aged 28, had been at sea since he was 15, like Harry. He was on the trawler *St. Dominic*.

Rita was accustomed to the idea of the men being away at sea for long periods, and coming ashore only for a few days at a time. So she knew that if she married Harry she would be coping with a home, and any children they might have, on her own for much of the year. But she loved Harry. Seamen took pride in their work, and Rita shared Harry's pride, participating in her husband's joys and sorrows like other seamen's wives.

In 1965 Harry and Rita were married at St Nicholas' Church on the Hessle High Road in Hull. Remarkably enough, although all the men in both families spent much of their lives at sea, they all managed to attend the wedding except for Michael Eddom, the bridegroom's younger brother, who was working on an ocean liner bound for India. The newlyweds rented a house on the Boulevard, near the docks in Hull.

Before long Harry was promoted to boatswain. And as soon as he had earned his mate's ticket he was appointed first mate on the *Ross Illustrious*, and went on a three-month trip to the fishing grounds off Newfoundland. But he was fortunate enough to be able to spend Christmas at home—the first Christmas since his marriage to Rita. They now had a baby daughter, Natalee.

Harry had intended to be home for the birth, which was expected around May 20, but the little girl kept her parents waiting until June 13, by which time her Dad was out at sea again, this time off Iceland.

At the end of 1967 Harry was appointed first mate of the *Ross Cleveland*, and sailed before New Year's Eve, to return 22 days later. On Saturday, January 20, 1968 he was setting off on his second trip on the trawler.

Dick Moore was settling in aboard the *Notts County*.

"They were a motley crew on the ship. Trawlermen are enormously superstitious, and always thinking about the most important thing—will we have good catches on this trip? I didn't know

Harry and Rita Eddom on their wedding day.

❑ Dark Winter—The Hull Daily Mail

a soul aboard. I'd never met any of them before. But I had the feeling that, in spite of the delay, most of them were pleased to be setting off to go fishing, and get the trip over with. I noticed one man who was particularly unfriendly to Frank and me when we came aboard from the tug. He was very aggressive, and snapped snide remarks at us. 'There's always one black sheep,' I thought to myself.

The men were working on various tasks to prepare for departure to Iceland, and getting the fishing gear ready. I thought it was best to keep a low profile while they were getting used to us, the new men aboard."

The skipper of the *Notts County* was 40-year-old George Burres. First mate was 36-year-old Barry Stokes, and the chief engineer, Brian Good, was about thirty. The second engineer was George Galbraith, who was about the same age as the skipper. Another officer was radio operator Joyce Aabert; he was the eldest of

Hessle High Road in Hull, where the trawler companies had their offices. St. Nicholas' Church, where the Eddoms were married, is also on the Hessle High Road.

❑ Dark Winter—The Hull Daily Mail

them, with thirty years' seafaring experience. They all lived in the Grimsby and Cleethorpes area. There were eight deckhands aboard, in addition to Dick Moore, plus two engine-room men.

Ahead of them was the journey to Iceland, up the east coast of Great Britain, through the Pentland Firth and then across the wild North Atlantic. The skipper had set course for the fishing grounds off the West Fjords of Iceland.

As they steamed towards Iceland, Dick felt he was beginning to fit in with the other crew members:

"Although they were a bit odd, most of them were pretty tough. All of them were likeable, except that one who just wouldn't leave me alone. But we all knew we had to work to-

Ross Cleveland *docking at Hull.*

❏ The Grimsby Telegraph

gether—otherwise our jobs would be far harder. Trawlermen soon get used to each other and become a team—like the Londoners in World War II, when the German air raids went on for months at a time, and they all learned to pull together.

It's something the British have in their nature. And seamen have the sea in their blood—some of them for generation after generation. On trawlers you learn to watch each other's backs. When you're together for weeks at a time, hard at work, maybe in bad weather, there's only one thing to do: stick together. If that doesn't happen, life becomes intolerable. Skippers always tried to keep the same crew on their ships, because they would work better together.

Everyone had the same goal in mind: good catches. The more fish, the more money. A seaman's minimum wage was £12 a week; when the ship was back in harbour, the trawler company calculated costs of fuel, provisions, fishing gear and so on. This was deducted from the total value of the catch, and the difference was shared out between the company and crew as "poundage." The captain generally received 10 percent, the head engineer a little less, and so on. The deckhands got the smallest share.

We were far from happy with our wages, especially since we sometimes worked eighteen hours a day when we were fishing. Then we had a six-hour rest period before we were due back on deck. This meant we often had no more than five hours' sleep a day for days at a time.

On the way to Iceland I was on duty for four hours, then had eight hours off. Some of the crew—the ones who didn't have to stand watch on the bridge—worked only from 8 a.m. to 5 p.m. But everyone was making ready for the coming effort of fishing, when working hours were longer, and the work pretty close to slavery.

I'd often sailed to the fishing grounds off Iceland in the two years I'd been on trawlers, but I'd never stepped ashore in Iceland. But I'd been ashore in Norway, where I had met a girl I thought I was in love with. We'd been writing to each other, and I thought about her a lot. I was determined to go back to Norway and see her again as soon as possible."

Harry Eddom had been earning a good deal more than Dick Moore in recent months. As first mate he received a 6.5% share of the value of the catch—£65 of every thousand pounds that went to the crew. On their last trip, the crew of the *Ross Cleveland* had shared out £5,000 after 22 days at sea, so Harry's share amounted to £325. The skipper had received £500, and even the deckhands had been paid more than £100, which was regarded as excellent for a deckhand in those days.

Dick was hoping for some such reward for his trip in the *Notts County*, so he could make a trip back to Norway to see his girl.

"In the two years I'd been on trawlers, I'd always thought of Iceland as being far away. In good visibility you could see the island as a smudge on the horizon. The fishing limit was 12 miles out, so we were a fair distance from the shore, even if we were right on the line.

Sometimes we talked about going ashore—that it might be fun. Some of the lads had already been to Iceland, especially those who were most experienced. Seamen like to go ashore, call at a pub, and hopefully meet some girls. Most of us were young, after all. But I'd heard alcohol was expensive in Iceland. And there was no beer! We'd also heard that the bars were open only at weekends.

It all seemed very remote.

All we trawlermen had was the sea and the sky, and the scream of the seagulls as they waited for whatever was thrown over the side, and in winter when the hours of daylight were few, we didn't have much chance to look up from our work. Our first priority was to fish, and earn a crust.

And then sail home with the catch—everyone hoping for a hefty payment of poundage—all looking forward to seeing their wives and children, girlfriends and other loved ones."

When the *Notts County* reached the fishing grounds off Iceland, the fishing was excellent. Skipper George Burres had found the best shoal and the best haddock they had seen for a long time.

"The old man's done it," the deckhands remarked to each other. They knew that the captain was a reliable man, and much respected. Aboard the trawler the atmosphere was cheerful, filled with anticipation. The crew all worked together to shoot the trawl, gut and clean the fish, and stow it in the hold.

"The better I work, the faster I work, the more money when I get home to Grimsby," was the thought in every man's mind. This was their heritage of the seamen's blood in their veins.

The crew worked hard and almost without respite—one at a time, they would dash down to the mess for a cup of tea and a bite to eat. Then it was time to put on the duck suit, gloves and sou'wester again and get out on deck to gut the fish, dealing with the sharp knife, the cold, slippery fish, scales and slime, as the vessel rolled from side to side. Beyond the gunwale there was nothing to be seen but the blackness of Icelandic midwinter and the rough and salty waves.

After eighteen hours of hard labour, the men stumbled into their bunks, stinking and exhausted. As soon as their sweaty heads touched the pillow, they were oblivious. And six hours later, another man would come to shake them awake and take his own turn to sleep. The newly awakened men were often confused for a while.

"What? Where am I? I was having such a nice dream. Am I due out on deck?" the deckhand would mumble when rudely wakened after a few hours' rest to face cold reality. He would have a quick cup of tea, then put on his woollen sweater and his cold, stinking duck suit. When the ship rolled heavily, they had to hang on by one hand, and use the other to get into their duck suit. Sometimes the vessel rolled so wildly that they had to cling on tight with both hands to keep their balance.

When they had been out at sea for about ten days, January came to an end. February, the coldest month of the year in Iceland, was about to begin.

Things didn't look good.

Over twenty British trawlers were fishing off the West Fjords of Iceland. When a skipper had found good fishing, he was careful not to send a word over the radio, so as not to bring all the other trawlers flocking to the same spot. George Burres, skipper of the *Notts County*, took care not to give away his location; he told radio operator Joyce Aabert not to contact other trawlers or send any message that might give a clue to where the ship was.

The radio operator was a veteran, and was not surprised by the orders. But he had been hearing worrying weather forecasts. The more Aabert heard over the radio, the more convinced he became that the *Notts County*'s excellent fishing was about to come to an end.

Dick Moore's mind was on how and when he could visit his girlfriend in Norway:

"I thought of my family, who lived in Brighton: my stepfather Jack, and my two sisters, Caroline and Ann. My mother was dead. I'd met my Norwegian girlfriend about three months before. We'd been fishing off the Norwegian coast, and were shooting the nets when I was hit on the head by one of the doors. I was knocked unconscious, and was taken into Honningsvaag in the far north of Norway with concussion. I was admitted to hospital, where I met my girlfriend, who was a nurse there.

I really liked her. I thought she felt the same way about me. When I left Norway we wrote, but now I was at sea off Iceland, far away from Norway. But not in my mind—any more than other fishermen when they think of their families and loved ones.

Considering how well we were fishing, I thought I'd have at least £80-90 poundage after the trip. Maybe even £100 or £150. I was daydreaming—those were good wages for a deckhand, but not riches. I was optimistic, thinking I could soon visit my girlfriend in Norway,

We'd already got about a hundred tons of fine Icelandic cod and haddock in the hold. I noticed the weather was deteriorating, but I didn't think it would make any difference to us. We all wanted to carry on fishing. We heard that the skipper had mentioned a gale warning. And I noticed that the swell was getting quite heavy and the ship rolling badly. The wind was also a lot stronger and was whistling loudly through the rigging.

We had a lot of trouble hauling in the trawl. The ship was rolling heavily, and men and loose objects were being tossed around."

The coastguard vessel *Odin*, which dealt with both Icelandic and British trawlers, had reached the West Fjords. In late January, Petur Sigurdsson, Director General of the Iceland Coastguard, had called Sigurdur Th. Arnason to a meeting. Sigurdur had spent years as mate and skipper on coastguard vessels, and now he was requested to take over as captain of the *Odin*, whose skipper, Gudmundur Kjærnested, was going abroad.

The *Odin* had sailed from Reykjavik on January 31. Sigurdur knew he had many difficult tasks ahead of him, as always in the Coastguard:

"The tour was eventful from the start. We started out sailing west to the Midnes Sea, between Sandgerdi and Hafnir in the southwest, and there we caught six small Icelandic boats fishing inside the limits, practically all at once. We escorted them in to Keflavik, where they all appeared in court that same day. We then went out to the Midnes Sea again and caught another five—some of them were the same ones we'd caught the first time around! They seemed to think the grass was greener on the other side of the fence.

Before we sailed for the West Fjords, we had apprehended eleven boats fishing illegally. We then sailed northwest, and transported some passengers from Isafjord to Sugandafjord, as the road was closed by snow. Then on into Önundarfjord."

It was February 3. Back in England, the loss of two trawlers was causing a public outcry. The *St. Romanus*, a 600-ton trawler from Hull, had sailed on January 10 for Lofoten in Norway. The

Iceland Coastguard vessel Odin.

trawler *St. Matthew* had reported hearing from the *St. Romanus* on January 13—but many days later it transpired that this was a misunderstanding; the ship that had contacted the *St. Matthew* was not the *St. Romanus*, but her sister ship, the *St. Andronicus*.

In fact, no one had heard from the *St. Romanus* since the day she sailed out of the Humber, except for an Icelandic boat, *Vikingur III* from Isafjord, which reported having heard a Mayday call from the *St. Romanus* on January 11. As the British trawler was hundreds of miles from Iceland, the boat's crew felt there was nothing they could do. They also gathered that the trawler had made contact with another British vessel, so they assumed that appropriate action had been taken.

When it later emerged that nothing had in fact been heard from the *St. Romanus* after January 11, the vessel was declared missing. There were twenty men aboard.

The air and sea search did not commence until January 26, and it yielded no result. It was not uncommon for British trawlers to maintain radio silence for many days at a time, and there was no radio operator aboard the *St. Romanus*, although the skipper, James Wheeldon, was qualified to operate the radio. The trawler was regarded as lost.

Tragedy overwhelmed the people of Hull—twenty fishermen had lost their lives.

And now another trawler was missing—the 658-ton *Kingston Peridot*, also from Hull, with a crew of twenty. She had sailed on the same day as the *St. Romanus*, 10 January. The last radio contact from the *Kingston Peridot* was at 10 a.m. on Friday, February 2, when she was west of Grimsey island, off Iceland's north coast.

Now the *Kingston Peridot* too was believed to have sunk!

Hull had lost 40 seamen. Seamen's wives and widows in the town planned to send a deputation to London, and wrote a letter of protest to Prime Minister Harold Wilson. They wanted a complete review of safety standards on British trawlers, and higher pay. They also demanded that every vessel should have a radio operator, that regular location reports should be required, and that inexperienced men should not be sent out to sea without training.

As the *Notts County*, the *Ross Cleveland* and the coastguard vessel *Odin* sailed off the West Fjords in early February, the people of Hull were overcome with grief and anger for the men who had gone down with the *St. Romanus* and *Kingston Peridot*. Dozens of women had lost their husbands, and yet more children were left fatherless. All the British media reported on the tragedies.

Mrs. Lilian Bilocca, a big woman who was the resolute and unflinching leader of the seamen's wives of Hull, had declared on February 3 that if anyone dared to try sailing out of harbour without a radio operator and an experienced crew, she would board the vessel herself. She would have to be dragged off by force unless the women's demands were met. Now everybody knew who Lillian Bilocca was—the media had dubbed her "Big Lil."

But the catalogue of tragedy was only beginning.

The working conditions of British trawlermen would be debated in Parliament. And the members of the House, like the whole British nation, would be horrified by the news from Iceland over the next few days.

Gale-force winds were forecast on the fishing grounds off Iceland, especially at the northwest, where between 20 and 30 British trawlers were fishing. For the next few days, in the British media the tragedy at sea off Iceland would even overshadow news of the Vietnam War.

On the *Ross Cleveland* the fishing had not been going well. Initially skipper Phil Gay had decided to fish off northeast Iceland, but abandoned this due to the weather conditions, and sailed westwards. A few days earlier, the ship's cook, 59-year-old William Howbrigg, had been taken seriously ill, and the ship had sailed in to Isafjord, the main town of the West Fjords, for him to receive medical attention. The town of Isafjord is located, not in the fjord of the same name, but by Skutulsfjord, one of the many fjords on the south side of the broad Isafjardardjup (Isafjord Bay) that cuts deeply into the West Fjords peninsula.

As the trawler sailed into the narrow harbour mouth at Isafjord, Harry Eddom looked out over the little town, surrounded by lofty mountains. In recent years he had often been to Isafjord, where he found the people hospitable and pleasant to deal with. He sometimes visited the home of policeman Kristjan Kristjansson, where he was plied with coffee and pancakes, and sometimes even seized the opportunity for a proper hot bath.

The Hull trawler Kingston Peridot.

The Hull trawler St. Romanus.

After putting the sick cook ashore at Isafjord, the *Ross Cleveland* had sailed for the off-shore fishing grounds. But now snow, gales and freezing temperatures made it impossible to continue, and the ship was once again making for Isafjord, for safe harbour.

Rita and Harry Eddom with their daughter Natalee, aged seven months.

❏ Dark Winter—The Hull Daily Mail

The coastguard vessel *Odin* was in Önundarfjord on the western side of the West Fjords peninsula; she was to take shelter there on Saturday evening and drop anchor. Radio operator Valdimar Jonsson was at his station aft of the bridge:

"I heard Isafjord Radio calling. The British trawler *Northern Prince* had sent out a PAN call for the trawler *Wyre Mariner*, which had sprung a leak. She was heading in to Isafjord. The PAN call was a sort of preliminary to a Mayday call. It meant the crew were in danger, but not in urgent need of assistance.

The *Odin* sailed to assist her, at full speed.

I called up the *Northern Prince* at 10:30 that evening, and told the radio operator that under the current conditions we expected to reach them at 1:30. But just before midnight the *Wyre Mariner* reported that she was one mile from where the Isafjord pilot

Valdimar Jonsson, radio operator on the coastguard vessel Odin.

could come aboard. We were in Isafjord Bay by then. Three quarters of an hour later, we heard from Isafjord Radio that the trawler had docked, and was no longer in need of assistance.

We noticed that the weather had deteriorated rapidly after we sailed north from Önundarfjord."

Sigurdur Arnason, skipper of the *Odin*, had listened to the Icelandic weather forecast that evening.

"The last forecast was very bad. At 10:15 we listened to the radio forecast on long wave. I decided to take shelter under the lee of Grænahlid, north of Isafjord, and wait there. There were 22 vessels there, mostly British trawlers."

Aboard the *Notts County*, Bill McPeak, the nineteen-year-old cook's mate, was trying to make sandwiches and tea for the men who had been at work out on deck, and were due to come below. The ship was rolling so wildly that he had great difficulty staying on his feet, and could hardly keep the food and teapots steady.

Dick Moore was exhausted after a long shift and days of hard labour. Fatigue and bad weather had overcome the thrill of good catches:

"All I wanted was a bit of rest. We were sailing into shelter to get out of the storm. I heard we were heading for Iceland, into some fjord, but I had no idea where. The skipper shouted out to us to abandon the trawl for the time being—get everything ship-shape—as we were going to seek shelter.

In fact we'd been fishing till the very last minute—as long as we could stay out there without men actually being washed over-board. It was really dangerous to be out on deck.

'Thank God,' we said. Conditions were hazardous, and the sea was wild, waves pounding over us, pouring over the bulwarks and flooding over everything. There was so much sea coming aboard that the scuppers could hardly clear it.

In spite of everything, I felt quite secure, knowing that the skipper was an experienced, reliable man, and the *Notts County* was a pretty good ship.

It was pitch black outside. The weather had been overcast that Saturday. I noticed it had started to snow heavily. The skipper was bringing the ship around, and she rolled even more wildly. Now we were heading into the fjord. Men were up on deck, battening down the hatches and putting equipment away.

Some got ready to go into the mess to eat, then to their bunks to rest after their long shift. But I wasn't so lucky. It was my watch.

Most of the men went into the mess in all their gear—duck suit, sea boots, the lot. Under the duck suit I was wearing two pairs of trousers, two jumpers and a jacket, and I had a scarf

*Nineteen-year-old Bill McPeak, cook's
mate on the* Notts County.

❏ Morgunblaðið

The Notts County *at sea.*

❏ Morgunblaðið

round my neck. You needed all those clothes—because when you're out on deck gutting fish you stand still most of the time. Water ran down the sou'wester and down the back of the duck suit. And the wind blew up underneath the open edge of the duck suit. You were protected from rain and sea, except for your face.

I took off my sou'wester and work gloves. The mess was furnished with sturdy tables and benches; the floor was rough tile. We had our tea and sandwiches; the ship was rolling so much we had to hold tight, not to fall off the benches."

On the Saturday night, ice was building up on the vessels in Isafjord Bay. All the British trawlers which could had sought shelter there, and some had even reached harbour at Isafjord.

Out in Isafjord Bay, it was snowing, with gale-force winds.

But, worst of all, the temperature had dropped to minus 10°C (about 20°F), and the temperature of the sea was minus 2°C (30°F). Ice started to accumulate on the superstructure of the vessels—inch by inch, ton by ton.

At 4 a.m., Valdimar Jonsson, radio operator on the *Odin*, was shaken awake with bad news: the vessel's main transmitting aerials, between the fore and aft masts, had come adrift. The weight of ice on them had proved too much, and no one could get up to the aerials to knock the ice off.

The ship's officers found it difficult to see other vessels on the radar, due to the build-up of ice; nearby ships which had taken shelter below Grænahlid were indistinct, and there was a risk of collision. Visibility was no more than 50 metres.

Valdimar was concerned:

"All my aerials, the wire aerials, had come adrift, and ice had built up on the microwave aerial. So our contact with Isafjord Radio was very poor. The British trawlers in Isafjord Bay had microwave equipment, and we couldn't monitor them at all well. They could be transmitting on two or three working wavelengths on microwave, but our equipment was almost exclusively tuned into 16, the VHF emergency frequency.

Shortly before midday, it was decided that the *Odin* would go north into the Jökul fjords, to avoid the risk of collision with other vessels under Grænahlid.

27

When ice builds up on the super-structure of a ship, it becomes less stable, and there is a risk of the vessel laying over on her side and sinking.

❏ Dark Winter—The Hull Daily Mail

A trawlerman chopping ice off the superstructure.

❏ Dark Winter—The Hull Daily Mail

I went up on the roof of the bridge, and pulled the aerials onto one of the bridge wings. I rolled them up into a bundle, and that way I managed to establish a fairly good connection with the coastguard radio. But on the emergency wavelength, 2182 KHz, I couldn't even reach Isafjord Radio. My transmitter wouldn't tune in to the bundles of wire out on the bridge wings.

So I thought I'd have to fix up some kind of wire so I could make contact with Isafjord. They didn't have a microwave station. The situation didn't look good."

Palmi Hlödversson, second mate on the *Odin*, was a dependable 26-year-old from Reykjavik, who had considerable seagoing experience. He had been a mate on coastguard vessels since 1965, and the last two years on *Odin*, so he was familiar with the vessel:

"The weather suddenly deteriorated when we sailed out of Önundarfjord into Isafjord Bay late on the Saturday evening. Ice piled up, and the temperature was about minus 10°C. The seawater washing over froze solid as soon as it hit the steel.

But the weather had been much worse under Snæfjallaströnd, opposite Isafjord. The wind was gusting at incredible speeds, and ice built up so fast there was nothing we could do. The icing on our radar scanners was so bad that they were quite useless. They were placed high up on the ship, and the only way you could clear them was to climb the ice-covered mast in that awful weather. The radar mast on top of the bridge was twice its usual diameter.

The aerial wires and stays were lying around all over the deck, because of the icing. We'd taken the wires, cut the fastenings off, and placed one end at the rear of the helicopter landing pad. The other end was passed down the funnel and into the radio cabin.

This meant we got through to Isafjord Radio on 2182 KHz."

Captain Sigurdur Arnason had managed to snatch a few hours' rest that night. Early that morning he returned to the bridge:

"When I got to the bridge, the mates said the radar was very poor because of the icing. We knew there were trawlers all around us. We could see the coast on the radar, but we couldn't discern the ships. We heard the British vessels chatting among themselves on two or three wavelengths, about this and that, and the weather. But we weren't monitoring them closely."

On Sunday morning Isafjord Bay, and in fact the whole of Iceland, was caught up in a freak storm. On the road between Isafjord and Hnifsdal, about five kilometres away, eleven people had been trapped in their cars. All over north Iceland and the West Fjords, roads were closed by the snow. In Siglufjord a family narrowly escaped when an avalanche struck their house.

Around Isafjord Bay, people were stuck inside their houses; the winds were so high that it was impossible to keep on your feet out of doors, and the blizzard was blinding.

In the harbours of Isafjord and nearby Bolungarvik, boats and trawlers were tossed about as if on the high seas.

Just before ten in the morning, the British trawler *Lord Howe* notified Isafjord Radio that another trawler, the *Boston Typhoon*, had slipped its moorings at Isafjord, and had probably run aground. But nobody knew where it could be in the blizzard. The crew could not see land, and there was no sighting of them. But since the trawler had been in harbour in the Pool when it broke loose, it should be easy enough to find when the weather died down. In hopes that the crew were safe, at Isafjord people remained where they were.

The *Lord Howe* informed Isafjord Radio that she intended to stay in contact with the grounded trawler. Rescue teams could do little to help in such wild weather conditions.

Meanwhile out on Isafjord Bay, where twenty trawlers and the coastguard vessel *Odin* were, conditions were steadily deteriorating. More and more ice built up on the vessels; they were in danger of becoming so top-heavy that they would turn turtle under the weight of the ice.

A radar scanner covered in ice.
❏ Dark Winter—
The Hull Daily Mail

* * *

As Valdimar Jonsson, radio operator on the *Odin*, tuned into the microwave frequency and listened to the British trawlermen, he heard how astonished they were to find themselves in such appalling weather in Isafjord Bay—where they had expected to be able to take shelter. But their main concern was the icing. They were as worried as the crew of *Odin*, who were also in serious difficulties.

Skipper Sigurdur on the *Odin* was uneasy:

"When I heard the news from Isafjord, I could hardly believe that a trawler that was tied up to the dock could have slipped her moorings. If people weren't safe in harbour, where were they safe? To make things worse, for a time nobody knew what had happened to the ship. The wind was so high, and the blizzard so thick, that there was nothing they could do."

Gudmundur Gudmundsson was chairman of the Isafjord chapter of the Life-Saving Association:

Winches sheathed in ice.
❑ Dark Winter—
The Hull Daily Mail

"I was sitting by the phone, at home at Silfurgata 7 in Isafjord, listening to the ships' wavelength, and monitoring all the communications as far as I could.

There was such a fierce gale blowing that you could hardly stand upright out of doors. You couldn't see the next house. Men with 100-ton boats were reluctant to try sailing into the harbour at Isafjord, because the harbour mouth is very narrow, and you can't navigate in on radar alone. I'd been a harbour pilot for six years, so I was familiar with the conditions.

I'd never seen such weather. The snow was pelting down, mostly driven horizontal by the wind, so you couldn't even get to the next house. And it was freezing cold."

The trawler *Notts County* had entered Isafjord Bay. Dick Moore was seriously worried:

"I'd got a bit of sleep that night, in brief snatches—the ship had been rolling heavily on the way to land. But it was bitterly cold outside—the chill crept into every nook and cranny of the ship.

When night fell the previous evening, the weather had deteriorated even more, with howling gales. It got colder and colder. I heard that a lot of British trawlers had gathered together and gone into the fjord. And we heard from other trawlers that they had ice building up.

The same was happening to us. 'What's happening—is the weather getting worse?' I thought. 'Aren't we supposed to be in shelter? In a fjord? Incredible.'

We'd been called out by the skipper over the tannoy:

'All hands on deck to clear the ice.'

A shiver ran down my back. Fear crept through me. What did it mean, what were we in for? What kind of a hell-hole were we in? What would happen to us? I didn't like the look of it.

When I got out on deck, I was met by the most incredible sight. In the dim daylight you could see the snow pouring down. All the deck lights were on; it was Christmassy, yet not! Everything was shrouded in ice. Masts, railings, portholes, winches, cables, bulkheads, hatches—everything was white. A floodlit ice sculpture bombarded by the waves in the middle of a blizzard. The lights cast an eerie light. I noticed that an inch-thick cable was now as big as a tree-trunk.

The trawler as it looked now didn't seem to be made of steel. At first it seemed both beautiful and unnerving. At the same time as I was seeing something that not many others have ever seen, I realised the danger we were in. The ship's movements were odd—it seemed far more sluggish than before. I found it difficult to keep my balance.

Beyond the gunwale, everything was white. I couldn't even see the waves. But I could feel them, because the ship was

33

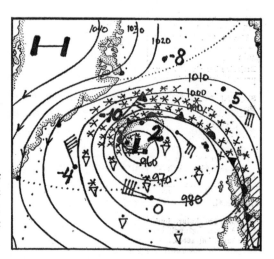

Weather conditions around midday on February 4, 1968, as shown on a meteorological map.

rolling wildly, tossing us back and forth on the slippery deck, and icy water cascaded over us.

The lights were almost blinding. I could both feel and hear the howling of the gale."

Sigurjon Hannesson, first mate on the *Odin*, was 32 years old, an experienced seafarer. He too was out in the storm as the coastguards fought to keep their vessel on an even keel. They had to navigate solely on instruments, to avoid running ashore or colliding with other ships:

"Once we got into the Jökul fjords, we ran before the wind, and managed to scrape the ice off the scanner of the lower radar. Palmi clambered up the ice-coated mast, and I followed to help him. It was a tough job. Palmi went up on the mast and I followed, holding him to the mast by the waist, while he scraped. Meanwhile the skipper turned against the storm, so the wind helped hold us fast to the mast.

And it worked. The radar started working better—for the time being, at least.

In the Jökul fjords the weather was slightly better than in Isafjord Bay."

At Isafjord, Gudmundur Gudmundsson was in touch with the headquarters of the Life-Saving Association in Reykjavik, to notify them of the situation:

"Usually when a dangerous situation arose out at sea I was in phone contact with Hannes Hafstein of the Life-Saving Association, who was in Reykjavik. I was the link between Hannes and the other rescue personnel.

I'd informed him of the situation in Isafjord Bay—I'd first spoken to him about the *Heidrun II*, IS 12, which had been moored at Bolungarvik. The engineer of the *Heidrun*, my old friend Rögnvaldur Sigurjonsson and his two sons, had managed to jump aboard the *Heidrun* as she slipped her moorings at Brjoturinn, a concrete jetty that was the main harbour structure at Bolungarvik.

The *Heidrun II*, which was a 153-ton boat, sailed out into the bay, heading for shelter in Isafjord. But by the time they sailed past Oshlid and approached the mouth of Skutulsfjord, where the town of Isafjord is located, the weather had grown so wild that they dared not try to sail into the fjord. The radar and depth sounder were both malfunctioning."

Captain Sigurdur on the *Odin* was in contact with the boat *Gudmundur Peturs IS 1*, in harbour at Isafjord.

"We asked the crew of the *Gudmundur Peturs* whether they could help the *Heidrun* get into harbour if we could escort her down to Prestabugt. They said that the harbour entrance was quite impassable. So the *Heidrun* stayed out in Isafjord Bay, intending to tie up to a light buoy they were going to put out."

Bad news was coming in from all over the West Fjords. During the night one of the worst storms in living memory had raged at Latrabjarg, Iceland's westernmost point. Thordur Jonsson at Latrabjarg had reported that at 2 a.m. a northerly gale had struck, with frost, snow and rough seas. The weather forecast indicated that worse was still to come. Buildings shook, anything that was not secured was swept away by the winds, and hailstones drummed on roofs. Windows that faced into the wind were in danger of breaking. The storm continued all night, and went on until around midday, when the wind speed dropped a little, down to force 12. At Latrabjarg, the farming family attempted to get to their livestock in nearby buildings; outside, it was impossible to stand upright in the wind. Shortly afterwards, the gale struck again with renewed force. Vehicles were blown about, and even indoors it was safest to hold on tight.

Thordur said the storm had raged without respite until the middle of the night, when it began to die down. The temperature of the sea was 1°C at Latrabjarg, but five nautical miles out at sea it was at freezing point. For seafarers, icing on the vessels was an inevitable risk.

It was nearly ten on Sunday night, and over 400 seamen were struggling to keep their vessels afloat in Isafjord Bay. Among them were the six men aboard the *Heidrun II* from Bolungarvik. The crew of the *Gudmundur Peturs* in Isafjord harbour were passing messages from the *Heidrun* to the *Odin*, asking the coastguard vessel to come to their aid, so they could take an accurate fix of their position. The *Heidrun* was tied up to a light buoy; they thought they were beneath Bjarnarnupur at the

An ice-laden trawler in early 1968.

❏ Vísir

mouth of the Jökul fjords. The connection was bad, so it was difficult to hear any more from the *Heidrun*. But the crew of the *Heidrun* were believed to be receiving other signals clearly.

Phil Gay, skipper of the *Ross Cleveland*, was the brother of Christine Smallbone, one of the women who were on their way to London to protest against the working conditions of trawlermen, after the tragic accidents off Iceland and elsewhere. She had no idea that her brother, as well as many relatives and friends on other trawlers, were in mortal danger in Icelandic waters. The people of Hull were still in shock after the last wave of accidents.

The trawlers in Isafjord Bay maintained contact among themselves, doing their best to help each other—especially since the radar equipment on the vessels was covered with ice and malfunctioning; some was quite useless.

Aboard the *Ross Cleveland*, the radar had been troublesome, and sometimes they had little or no idea of their position. Members of the crew had to climb up onto the bridge roof to knock

the ice off the radar scanner. The *Ross Cleveland* had been passing on information to other vessels. Harry was on the bridge, and
skipper Phil Gay had been in touch with George Burres on the
Notts County. They compared notes on the locations of the ships.

Phil Gay had considered various options to try to get the
trawler out of these appalling conditions. The radio operator on the
Ross Cleveland sent a message: "The weather is too bad for us to
go south." The radio operator on the trawler *Leonis*, sister ship of
the *Ross Cleveland*, was one of those who received the message.

First mate Harry Eddom was on duty:
"We were only two or three miles from the 3,000-foot walls of
the fjord. We should have been safe as houses."

The radar of the *Notts County* had long since ceased to func-
tion. One radar receiver had failed on the Sunday morning; the
other was already out of order.

Captain Burres was anxious, but this was not obvious, except
perhaps to radio operator Joyce Aabert, who had known him for
a long time. They worked in close proximity to each other—Burres on the bridge, Aabert in the radio cabin behind it.

No one around the *Notts County*, and probably no one aboard
any of the 22 British trawlers in Isafjord Bay, had ever seen anything like the storm they were caught up in. Only a month before, Dick Moore had been at sea in one of the worst storms of
the century in the British Isles:

"I'd been in a howling storm on the trawler *Ross Lynx* in the
North Sea east of Scotland. The weather caused enormous damage in Scotland, and there were a number of deaths. The waves
were 35 to 45 feet high.

But the situation seemed worse now. It was appalling. We
were in sub-zero temperatures, with ice building up. Seamen are

Joyce Aabert, radio operator on the Notts County.

❏ Morgunblaðið

used to storms and heavy seas, but storm and icing is far, far worse. You're fighting a desperate battle with the forces of nature, which you feel are trying to sink the ship by the sheer weight of the ice building up.

We'd never experienced anything like it.

The waves washed over the ship in an icy spray, which froze solid as soon as it hit the vessel. I felt I was seeing the sea, snow, wind and the chilling subzero temperatures build up ice with incredible speed.

More and more, thicker and thicker.

The heavy ice built up steadily on the superstructure of the trawler. There was a growing risk of the vessel turning turtle. I was scared stiff, and my heart was hammering in my chest—not only from the effort of knocking off the ice, but also from sheer fear. The crew had no idea what would happen next. Even in the eyes of the most experienced seamen aboard you could see despair."

The crews of the trawlers in Isafjord Bay had been occupied in chopping ice off their vessels almost continuously for more than 12 hours. They soon became tired, and so they took turns at the work. The skippers turned their vessel into the wind, or alternatively turned tail to wind and sailed at low speeds. And they tried to choose the most favourable times to send the men out on deck to knock and hammer the ice off the superstructure.

The trawler *Kingston Andalusite*, sister ship of the recently lost *Kingston Peridot*, was about four hundred metres from the *Ross Cleveland*. The ships were sailing at half speed into the wind. They had stuck together in the blizzard, and the skippers had conferred and shared advice. A short time earlier, the *Ross Cleveland*'s radar had failed, and Len Whur, skipper of the *Kingston Andalusite*, had given Philip Gay advice on the course to steer.

Aboard the *Ross Cleveland*, ice was being chopped off the ship. The trawler was about two nautical miles north of Arnarnes—a headland at the south of Isafjord Bay, between Skutulsfjord and Alftafjord. Captain Gay tried, like the other skippers, to sail back and forth in the same area of sea.

It was past 10 p.m. Harry Eddom was one of the men who went out on deck to deal with the icing. The clearing of the radar scanner had been largely his work:

"I lurched up to clear the radar scanner of ice, and came back to the bridge. We began to "dodge"—trying to get under the cover of the fjord walls. I had sent two lads, Barry Rogers and Maurice Swain, to my own berth to get their heads down until I needed them." Since Harry's cabin was amidships, it would be easier for him to call down to the men than if they went to their own cabins, which were forward.

"Suddenly the wind caught us and we went over at about 45 degrees. No one was taking unnecessary risks—it was sheer bad luck.

I shouted down to the engine room for full speed, but it was no good. We fought to get her back up again, but she wouldn't come."

The *Ross Cleveland* had been sailing at half speed. Skipper Gay radioed Skipper Whur on the *Kingston Andalusite*. "Help me, Len, we're going over!"

"Put the engines on full speed ahead, Phil, follow us," Whur shouted into the radio. He had caught a glimpse of the *Ross Cleveland*'s navigation lights through the snowstorm.

Skipper Gay rang "full speed ahead" on the engine-room telegraph.

The two engineers gave the ship all the power they could.

The skipper tried to bring the ship around into the wind by turning hard to starboard. Harry heard Barry Rogers coming up the companionway:

"She just took a sea. We gave her everything we'd got, but she just wouldn't come. She wouldn't bring her head back into the wind. I saw we were going. I heard the lads down below panicking. Most of them just didn't stand a chance." The *Ross Cleveland* lay over on her side.

Phil Gay realized what was happening. He called over the radio:

"We're going. I'm going. Give our love to our wives and families."

Aboard the other British trawlers, those who heard the stoic voice of the skipper—who clearly spoke in the knowledge that these would be his last words in this life—felt a shiver down the spine. One of them was Joyce Aabert, radio operator on the *Notts County*. Deeply affected by the words spoken by the skipper from Hull, no one could speak.

"Will the ice capsize us as well?" was in every mind.

Len Whur had seen the navigation lights of the *Ross Cleveland*. To his horror he saw the ship keel over on her side. The red lights on the port side vanished. Then there were no lights. He went back to the radio and called "Ross Cleveland, *Ross Cleveland*, are you there? Come in, please!"

But there was no reply. The trawler was fading from the radar screen.

Harry Eddom had been on the starboard side of the bridge. He and Barry Rogers just managed to struggle out onto the bridge wing before the ship lay right over on her port side, which would have trapped them on the bridge with no hope of escape:

"Wally Hewitt, the bo'sun, just managed to throw a life raft into the sea when the ship went over. She sank in six or seven seconds. Most of the crew could never have known what happened.

She dipped herself and I went right under. I suppose it was the shock of the water . . . I passed out."

The crew of the coastguard vessel *Odin* did not hear what was happening, because they were not monitoring the wavelength used by Philip Gay.

Aboard the *Notts County*, news of the fate of the *Ross Cleveland* spread like wildfire. Dick Moore, who had gone down to the mess for a rest, heard what was happening. News was passed down from the bridge every time something was heard over the radio:

"We'd heard that the *Ross Cleveland* was icing up dangerously. Our skipper, George Burres, had been in frequent contact with her. And I knew the *Ross Cleveland* had been helping us out with finding our position.

First I heard that the *Ross Cleveland* was listing badly. And almost immediately afterwards that she was going down.

It was like a cold slap in the face. Our countrymen, who had been struggling just like us, were being flung into the terrifying, icy sea. They were dying for sure. There was nothing we could do to help them. They hadn't a hope of survival in those conditions.

My heart was racing. My mouth was dry. I got goose-flesh thinking of all those seamen from the Humber, most of them family men, going down with their ship or fighting for their lives in the freezing-cold sea.

And now we were like blind kittens—we had no way of telling where we were, or where we were going."

Harry was regaining consciousness after passing out when the *Ross Cleveland* sank. He found himself in pitch darkness aboard a life raft with Barry Rogers, an 18-year-old sparehand, and Walter Hewitt, a 30-year-old boatswain. Both were, like Harry, from Hull.

"When I came to I was inside the raft with two of my mates, who must have dragged me aboard." Somehow the raft had got away from the foundering ship. Harry, who had been on duty, was warmly dressed, but "Wally was wearing only a shirt, trousers and gumboots, and the lad a tee-shirt and underpants."

The flaps of the life raft had been torn in the turmoil and a lot of water had washed inside. The shipwrecked men looked around for something to bale with and found an old can. They also used one of Wally's boots. As fast as they could bale, the waves washed over the life-raft and more water poured in.

The three men in the life raft had suffered a huge shock when they found themselves in the chilly sea, which was close to freezing point—especially the boatswain and sparehand, who had been below, woken up only lightly dressed, and managed with difficulty to make their way out of the foundering trawler alive. In some unfathomable way they had succeeded in launching the life raft and getting aboard.

Barry, still a teenager, and Wally, a married man with four children, started to shiver with cold. Like Harry, they tried to keep their heads in the darkness and heavy seas, in their tiny craft over which they had no control in the storm.

Nobody had any idea that they had managed to board the life raft—it was thought to be impossible that anybody could have survived.

The *Kingston Andalusite* notified *Odin* that she had "lost radar contact with the *Ross Cleveland*," but did not specify that the crew of the trawler believed the *Ross Cleveland* had capsized. So the coastguard crew were not much the wiser. Skipper Sigurdur interpreted the message to mean that they were being plagued by the same problem as before—that the radar was rendered useless by ice.

Dick Moore was back on the deck of the *Notts County*. The ship had been turned head to wind at slow speed.

"The snow was falling so thickly, and the wind was so strong, that I felt I could only see six inches in front of my face. If it hadn't been for the deck lights I would have been completely blinded. I wouldn't have seen a thing for the darkness and snow.

I grew more and more fearful after I heard about the *Ross Cleveland*. The storms and disasters I'd experienced at sea before could scare anyone, but they were nothing compared to this.

The situation was out of our control. It was the frost and the storm that were in charge."

Aboard the *Notts County*, the men were chopping and hammering at the ice. But the vessel had only four ice axes. When more men were at work, some battered at the ice with hammers and marlin spikes—used for splicing cables—and other metal implements. Dick was soon finding the physical effort intolerable:

"Holding on with one hand, trying to keep your balance on the ice-sheathed deck, and banging away at the ice with all your might, was no joke. Men went flying on the slippery deck—sometimes several at a time when the ship took a good dip. We used whatever we could to hammer the ice off the ship—any bit of metal, even a length of piping. Anything that would break the ice.

Lumps of ice slipped about—sometimes you had to jump out of their way when someone else had knocked off a hefty chunk. And hunks of ice were tumbling down from the mast and the upper deck, too, so you had to have your wits about you. It was wearing. But the worst thing of all was the fear—that made us even more exhausted. We were close to collapse, fighting for our lives.

Most of us were on the point of giving up. When we sailed into Isafjord Bay, many of the men had already been on duty for eighteen hours, working hard all the time, as the fishing was good. Before long, this new task had to be done—another eighteen hours, after only a brief rest. I no longer knew what day it was, or how much time had passed.

The situation was looking more and more alarming. We were aware of each other's growing fear and anxiety. How long can this go on? Will we survive?

It was like another world. But we had to go on—chopping, chopping desperately, at the ice. We had no time to think of the cold and exhaustion.

I was quite numb by now—I couldn't feel my body at all. I hacked automatically at the ice. 'You've got to go on. Don't sit down,' I thought. 'Don't do this! Don't do that!' I heard my shipmates shouting at each other.

I could feel the rising desperation of the crew. When you felt another man's despair, it was catching."

The coastguard vessel *Odin* was on her way to the place where the *Heidrun II* was supposed to be. Skipper Sigurdur was far from happy with the way the *Odin* was rolling and pitching in the waves:

"Shortly before we reached the place we thought the *Heidrun* was, I felt the storm intensify even more. I could hardly keep steerage on the ship.

We were travelling slowly, but she tended to drift off the course we'd set. We thought we'd got a sighting of the *Heidrun* on the radar, about a nautical mile south of the Bjarnarnupur headland. We approached the sighting, but we couldn't be sure it was her. We gave them our position, anyway, and asked the crew over the radio to switch their floodlights on.

We sailed around leeward of the vessel, but then we had to look right into the storm. We could just cope with peering into the blizzard. We either had the windows open, or stood out on the bridge wings."

Second mate Palmi Hlödversson was up in the *Odin's* wheelhouse:

"I was at the radar screen in the chartroom when Sigurdur called from the bridge:

'She's shining her lights on us!'

We were approaching a ship. I knew the crew of the *Heidrun* had been asked to switch the floodlights on as we approached. I looked out through the window of the bridge, but all I could see were lights. I couldn't make out what vessel it was. When they redirected the floodlights into the snow, there was a bright light around the rays, so it was almost blinding. There was no way to tell who they were."

Skipper Sigurdur felt conditions were too bad for any further action:

"Our Kelvin Hughes radar equipment was giving a poor picture, and the Sperry radar had cut out due to the icing. Because of the risk of collision, and the safety of my vessel, I thought of sailing out of Isafjord Bay and riding out the storm. I expected violent weather, but at least there would be no risk of running aground. We were coming to see that the weather was actually worst there, under Bjarnarnupur. Since the radio connection with the *Heidrun* was poor, we decided to send a blind message to them to sail west of Bjarnanupur. Although we couldn't hear them, we hoped they could hear us, and sent the message."

Aboard the *Notts County*, Dick thought to himself that he had never been so tired, nor so frightened. But things would get even worse:

"The skipper had kept the trawler moving slowly before the storm for some time while we hammered at the ice. He was heaving to, hoping we weren't too close to shore. The ice kept on accumulating as fast as we removed it. I imagined the ice we hadn't managed to get rid of would be even thicker when the skipper turned the ship's bow into the wind again.

I'd gone into the mess. It was a welcome break. I tried to get a seat and calm myself down a bit—I was dazed and trembling with exhaustion and fear. I had some tea. As I lifted the mug, I realised what a poor physical state I was in. My hands were shaking so much I could hardly hold the mug. But my hands soon warmed up. I didn't feel any calmer, though.

In the mess, the men were so nervous they had started snapping and grumbling at each other over the most unimportant things.

'That's my mug!' 'That's my sandwich!' 'Isn't that my place?'

Usually, we'd have laughed. But not now. We were at the end of our tether.

There we were, together. We would share the same fate. We were the same group of men who had worked so well together on the trawl.

'We're going to die,' I thought, knowing that my shipmates felt the same way. 'We're all going to die.'

We could hear over the loudspeaker what was happening on the radio up on the bridge. I could hear the captain and Aabert the wireless operator talking to other British trawlers. They were in just the same situation. It was discouraging. We heard that the main problem was with fixing a location. If you didn't know where you were, there was a greater risk of running aground. No one wanted his ship to break up on the rocky Icelandic coast. In this weather, no one could survive.

The radar scanners were mostly encased in ice and pretty useless.

But, when you heard from other trawlers, you knew you weren't alone. If something happened to us, maybe the others could come to the rescue. But, on the other hand, everybody was in much the same situation. Although the ships could communicate by radio, they couldn't see each other.

Dozens of British trawlers were caught in these freak conditions.

I thought of our countrymen who had been lucky enough to reach safe harbour at Isafjord. I was expecting the skipper to turn the ship and call us out on deck again to clear the ice. Everybody sat still, like condemned men.

Suddenly there was a shattering din, like a screeching noise, and a terrific jolt. For a second we exchanged terrified looks. My shipmates' frightened eyes were as big as saucers.

What was happening?

We were thrown off balance. Men who were sitting side by side were flung together, and some knocked against the bulkheads. Those standing were thrown to the deck.

From the galley there was a crash of crockery smashing. Everything on the tables was knocked over, or onto the deck. It was like a horror film. I found the screeching noise weird.

The exhausted men exchanged looks again in astonishment. For a few moments, they seemed to be coming out of their trance. Fear changed into curiosity.

Was it good or bad? Chaos reigned.

Suddenly the skipper's voice came over the loudspeaker:

'We've run aground!'

Curiosity gave way to disappointment, disappointment to terror. We were all paralyzed with fear."

In one corner of the mess sat a deckhand in his fifties, with his hands clasped together. He had a woolly hat on his head. Cold sweat poured from under the hat, down his forehead and over his weathered cheeks and swollen nose. His unfocused eyes indicated that he was giving up—that he was leaving this world in his mind, although his heart was beating madly. The motionless man seemed suddenly to be making his peace with God and man—having accepted that it was his time to go. . .

Dick heard the engine-room door open. The engineers were shouting:

"'The engine room is flooding!' called second engineer Galbraith.

The lights were going out—every light—every last gleam. And the engines were grinding to a halt with an eerie knocking sound, that changed into ticking, then faded and died away. Silence.

It was dark. I couldn't see anything—just hear.

I heard the voices of my shipmates and the sound of their boots on the mucky floor—sounds you never normally hear when the engines are running and the generators are on. The voices of my mates, and the rustling of their wet duck suits, became clearer than before in the darkness and silence. But as soon as the engines fell silent, there was a wild howling from outside. It was like being in a house on a bare plain, with the wind roaring and banging outside.

Now I could no longer see the fear in the crew's faces. But I could hear it. It was almost palpable. We were horrified.

'Out, out, out,' I thought. We felt our way to the door out onto the deck. Someone opened the bulkhead door, and we heard the overwhelming shrieking of the elements.

'What was that?' I thought. I was ready for anything—even finding myself in the cold sea. I put my hat on, and then my sou'wester, but I could feel the chilly air that blew in, biting at my cheeks. You could feel needles of frost in the air.

But what was that noise?

I couldn't see where I was going, and I knocked my knee against the coaming in the doorway, then stumbled out on deck. I heard the most unexpected and terrifying sounds I'd ever heard in nature.

A howling, screeching, shattering din. The ship was vibrating with the wind. I thought it was like being out on a runway with ten jet planes taking off at once. The air seemed to be tearing apart.

And the sound didn't die down. It went on and on—without pause. I put my hands over my ears; I felt thousands of ice-needles pricking my face, held my head down and tried to keep my balance on the ice. It was hard to breathe.

How could this be happening?

This howling gale had to be blowing off the nearby shore, or . . . I just couldn't understand it. It was as if the mountains themselves were shrieking and roaring.

But what was even worse was the noise the ship itself was making: crunching and banging, a sinister groaning of steel. I would never have imagined that this sturdy vessel could make such sounds. The trawler was settling on the rocks—or was it tearing itself apart, with us aboard?

Where on earth were we?"

Radio operator Joyce Aabert hastily sent a message: "Mayday! Mayday! Mayday!"

Captain Burres was not sure of the exact location of the ship, but he had a rough idea of where they had run aground. Aabert contacted nearby trawlers, and they passed the message on to the coastguard vessel *Odin*.

It was time for action. A British trawler had run aground off Snæfjallaströnd, an uninhabited region at the north side of Isafjord Bay. There was no way to attempt a rescue from land, and the coastguard vessel's radar equipment was so heavily coated in ice that it was impossible to set off at once to help the stranded ship.

Once more, second mate Palmi was in the front line. Again he put on his gloves, took his ice axe and a parallel rule, and clambered up the mast in the wild storm:

"Nobody felt able to climb the mast but me. It was like climbing a giant icicle. The footholds on the mast were buried in ice, so I had to cut hand- and footholds. When I got up the mast, it helped me to have the wind at my back, because Skipper Sigurdur had turned the ship stern to wind. The steps were on the aft side, so the wind held me closer to the icy mast. Once I'd cut my way up to the lower radar scanner, I had a more difficult task in store: getting the ice off the scanner itself. You couldn't use metal on it, because it was a delicate mechanism. I'd taken a plastic parallel rule—which is two rulers joined together by metal plates, used for plotting a course. First I tried making a hole, so I could get to the metal of the scanner. It took time. When I'd got through the ice, I pried it away with the parallel rule.

It worked, and the radar started working again. But it was hopeless to try climbing up to the big radar scanner at the top of the mast. You couldn't get up there in that weather. The lower scanner was halfway up the mast."

The *Odin's* engines were brought up to full speed.

Skipper Sigurdur was wondering what had happened to *Heidrun II* from Bolungarvik:

"On our way to the stranded ship, we thought we saw a boat on the radar, 2.7 nautical miles from the Bjarnarnupur headland, which we thought might be the *Heidrun*. We couldn't contact the boat, but we decided to send another blind message to the *Heidrun*, to go west of Bjarnarnupur, where the storm didn't seem to be quite so bad. We asked the boat to use its emergency transmitter, and transmit on frequency 2182 kHz. We didn't hear anything on that frequency, but they could have transmitted something. We knew our equipment wasn't reliable, as it was malfunctioning due to the ice."

Aboard the *Notts County*, chaos reigned. Like his shipmates, Dick was considering what to do:

"The engineer had managed to rig up some emergency lighting for the time being.

I noticed the seawater was beginning to wash over the deck. The waves were reaching us, up on the ship. I had the feeling we were sinking.

'Crew to the lifeboats,' someone shouted. I didn't hear whether it was the skipper. The men were putting on their life vests."

* * *

The men aboard the *Notts County*, some of them with decades of seagoing experience, felt the ship moving strangely and heard weird noises, the kind they might only have heard in horror films. Every time a wave washed under the ship, they heard the chilling cracking of the steel hull, which was being crushed on the rocks as this 400-ton vessel settled down on her belly on the sea floor.

The crew were speechless as they listened to the sinister groaning of the ship's hull, superstructure, derricks, winches and other metal structures in the howling gale, and the sea, at around freezing point or below, sprayed over the ship, seeping into every nook and cranny. The spray flew at such speed that each tiny drop froze to become a stinging needle of ice before it struck a man's face or other exposed skin.

Dick felt the ship was breaking up:

"Everything seemed to be tearing apart. We heard loud, screeching, crunching sounds. The ship had struck something, but what was it? A cliff, a skerry, rocks?

Aboard the ship, despair reigned—total chaos. Everybody wanted to get away.

'Get away from the ship, away from the ship!' men were shouting. 'Where are the life rafts?'

We were coming to understand what had happened.

'Abandon ship,' shouted the skipper. It seemed to me that the ship was going down with us aboard. I felt overwhelming fear around me.

All we could think of were the life rafts. One of them was on the windward side, aft. We threw it out. Initially, everything seemed to be all right. The raft inflated as soon as it went over, pulling the nylon cord that was fixed to the ship. But when the in-flated raft floated on the waves beside the ship, it was suddenly swept up by a gust of wind.

I couldn't believe my eyes. In a split second the raft flew up, over the bulwark and up to the superstructure. We watched in horror. There was nothing we could do. The raft went on—the howling, screeching storm lifted the life raft right up over the boat deck and over the superstructure. That heavy raft floated like a balloon. Then it tugged at the rope that held it to the ship, and broke like a piece of thread. The raft was gone—over the ship, into the terrifying darkness beyond.

We moved over to the leeward side, where there was another inflatable life raft. Now at least we were in the shelter of the superstructure. The raft inflated, but we found ourselves in difficulty. We pulled the raft towards the bridge, so we would have the best shelter. The raft was tossed around in the wind and waves. We had to do something to keep it steady, so the men could jump down into it."

Deckhand Robert Bowie, the man who had made hostile remarks to Dick and the other new hand when they boarded the ship in the Humber at the start of the tour, volunteered to jump overboard, to try to control the wild rolling of the life raft.

"One of us will have to try to keep the raft steady while the others jump aboard," he said. He jumped down into the raft and lay down on his back inside the life raft, under the canopy, with his arms and legs spread to try and keep the raft as flat as possible.

Dick observed one of his shipmates holding onto the bulwark as he tried to climb down into the raft:

"He had one foot on the raft when a massive squall struck. The raft suddenly seemed to dip. I reached out to grab the man who was getting down into the raft. He had to let go of the bulwark to jump down into the raft. He seemed to be hanging by his fingertips. The life raft was capsizing. The wind lifted the raft, and Robert Bowie was trapped inside the raft, under the canopy.

I grabbed the man who was climbing down into the life raft by his clothes, and held on like grim death. He very nearly went the same way as Robert. Some of the crew came and helped me get him back aboard.

Robert was under the life raft in the icy sea. We couldn't get hold of the raft. It was tied to the ship. But the waves and the storm took control. The raft drifted aft of the ship. The sea washed over the icy deck from time to time. It was hard to keep your balance; one man after another lost his footing and was washed up the deck by the waves breaking over the side.

We could hear Robert's despairing cries.

I felt a shiver down my spine as I thought of him struggling down there in the raft, in the chilly, salty sea in the dark. I could feel my heart hammering away, not just from exertion, but also from fear.

We all pulled on the rope as hard as we could. 'We've got to get him back on board!' the men shouted, panting with exhaustion. The gale made such a racket that we could hardly hear each other, except by shouting in the ear of the next man.

They hauled and shouted:

'Together, lads! Pull now!' again and again, and again.

We had to face the fact that, the more time that passed, the more chance there was our shipmate would die.

Robert shouted: 'Help! Get me back on board, get me back on board!'

I was close to tears, listening to his desperate cries. But we couldn't pull the life raft to us. We were no match for the forces of nature. Even upside down, the life raft caught the wind. It was like struggling with a gigantic inflated kite. The high winds, the snow and the power of the waves were too much for us.

Sometimes we managed to pull it a few feet toward us, but we could never get hold of the actual life raft.

'Help! Get me out of here!' he wailed.

I'd never known a battle of life and death before. Robert's voice gradually faded. He was clearly at the end of his powers."

The officers on the *Odin* discussed what they should do when they reached the stranded *Notts County* off Snæfjallaströnd. Valdimar heard a message on the Isafjord Radio.

News had been received that the crew of the *Notts County* were attempting to abandon ship. This was regarded as unwise on their part—they were simply inviting death. Experience had shown, over the years, that it was safest to remain aboard a stranded vessel—at least for the time being.

Isafjord Radio also passed on the information that the trawlers *Kingston Almondine* and *Kingston Andalusite* were near the stranded vessel.

Valdimar contacted the *Kingston Andalusite*, and learned that the *Notts County* had run aground about two nautical miles from the point of Bjarnanupur, and six from Skutulsfjord, where the town of Isafjord stands.

The *Odin* approached the place where the trawler was aground. A northeasterly storm battered the vessel, with high offshore winds, and a blinding blizzard. Visibility was almost nil, and the vessel had to navigate on instruments alone. Valdimar tried to raise the *Notts County*, but without success.

Second mate Palmi peered at the radar screen on the bridge, hoping to spot the stranded vessel:

"The image on the radar screen was consistent with the charts. But after quite some time we spotted something that seemed to be a little headland that shouldn't have been there, according to the charts. We concluded that it must be the ship. We realized that the only hope for those trawlermen was for us to get to them and rescue them. But there was nothing we could do in that weather. The crew were tired and nervous.

'Can we save them?' was what every man was thinking. Most of the coastguard crew had been awake for much of the last 24 hours, taking turns at chopping ice off the superstructure—not only the deck crew but engineers and engine-room crew, too—everyone lent a hand. We would take a rest from time to time, go into the mess for some coffee, and to warm up. You couldn't stay out on deck for long—it was just too cold, and when you got tired you couldn't work as well.

We changed places frequently."

The location of the stranded ship was now, finally, known with some accuracy. Valdimar transmitted to Isafjord Radio:

"When the mates had fixed the location, we sent the information to Isafjord—that the ship had run aground off Snæfjallaströnd, seven-and-a-half nautical miles off Ædey island. The trawler seemed to have stranded off the deserted farm of Sandeyri.

But I couldn't raise the men aboard the ship. As we had heard that they were trying to abandon ship, we had calculated that the survivors would be carried down towards the area between Skutulsfjord and Skötufjord. I passed this information on to Isafjord Radio too.

The storm raged on. Everything that touched the ship froze solid, whether sea water or snow. As soon as ice began to build up on the radar scanner, the picture began to blur on the screen in the bridge. We could hardly even see our immediate surroundings."

The message from the *Odin* had reached Gudmundur Gudmundsson and his men at the Life-Saving Association in Isafjord. Via Isafjord Radio they asked the coastguard whether they could help in any way with rescuing the men off the *Notts County*. After consulting with his officers, Valdimar replied that the wind was blowing at force 10 to 11 at the site, and that land-based rescuers could not do anything at present. Gudmundur was not happy with the situation:

"Around twelve-thirty I heard the *Heidrun* on the boat frequency. Rögnvaldur did not report any immediate danger on board. Although he was employed as an engineer, he had his skipper's ticket, and he'd been first mate on a boat with me. We'd heard that the *Ross Cleveland* had gone down, and that the *Odin* was in trouble due to icing. We contacted people on the farms between Skutulsfjord and Skötufjord."

The crew of the *Notts County* were still desperately trying to haul the life raft, and deckhand Robert Bowie, back on board the trawler. Dick was close to tears:

"We kept trying, and trying, but we were always slipping on the ice. As the sea was far up the sides of the ship, it washed over us, or to our feet, now and then. The conditions were so appalling that we were almost paralyzed with fear. Men were washed to and fro. Sometimes they stood up, but fell down again at once when the sea washed over. And it didn't help that we couldn't see what we were doing.

After a long battle with the life raft, when we were so exhausted we were close to giving up, the life raft floated closer to us. I suddenly thought of the filleting knives, which were close by.

'If we cut a hole in the raft, it will deflate,' I said. 'Then it won't catch the wind so much, and it will be easier to get it aboard.'

I got a knife. When I was within reach of the raft I stretched out with the knife in my hand. I stabbed forcefully into the raft, and cut it. Others tried to do the same.

To our surprise this didn't seem to make any difference. The raft hardly seemed to deflate at all—we then realized this was because it was divided up into a lot of separate compartments. If you cut one compartment, the others stayed inflated. It was a safety measure—so that the raft wouldn't sink if it struck something sharp.

The piercing cries of our shipmate cut me to the heart.

'How the hell can we get him back on board?' the men were asking. The poor man was helpless, and he was begging us to save him. We'd hauled and hauled and hauled on the rope. All for nothing.

Suddenly I realised I couldn't hear Robert's voice anymore. We knew that his struggle was over. His strength had run out.

We stood there, exhausted.

'I'm going to die here,' I thought to myself."

A short distance offshore from the grounded vessel was the *Odin*. The crew had a hard time keeping the ship on an even keel. First mate Sigurjon had never experienced anything like it:

"The weather was so appalling that it was every man for himself. And we could hardly see a thing. The scanner of the bigger radar set was supposed to withstand 80 knots wind speed, but it had been cutting out intermittently, due to the weather.

The temperature was minus 12°C, and what's more, even the sea temperature was minus 1.5 degrees! All the spray that washed over the deck froze solid. The blizzard was blinding. But it was the seawater that led to the build-up of ice, not the snow.

The *Odin* was listing at an angle of 30 to 45 degrees, with the bulwarks half-submerged. On the leeward side, the men were at work continuously, hammering the ice off the superstructure. Then the ship was turned around, and the other side was cleared. As we knocked the ice off, we didn't have to sweep it overboard; the deck was at such a steep angle that the ice fell into the sea on its own—off the bridge, the railing, or wherever.

We had to keep on hacking at the ice, to try to keep the ship on an even keel. We used whatever came to hand. If we hadn't done so, the ship couldn't have survived that storm. We were saving our ship, and ourselves. I had never known anything like it before."

Seventeen-year-old Torfi Geirmundsson from Reykjavik was a crewman on the *Odin*. He had never seen such weather:

"The *Odin* looked to me as if it was hardly keeping afloat, due to the icing. Several of us lads had tried to go forward when the ship was keeling over sharply. But as soon as we got out on the fore deck the gale slung us up against the rail. We couldn't stay on our feet. The ice built up so fast you couldn't let up for a minute. The only way you could chop the ice off was to stay on the leeward side."

For some reason the trawler *Kingston Andalusite* notified the *Odin* that the last life raft had left the *Notts County*. In fact the captain was still aboard, and had requested assistance from the *Ross Rodney*.

The coastguards aboard the *Odin*, and the members of the Life-Saving Association in Isafjord Bay, did not know whether any of the *Notts County*'s crew had managed to escape into the life rafts. Were some of the crew still aboard? Were they all alive? In the thick blizzard, it was impossible to try to trace life rafts, without having any idea of where they might be drifting. All that could be done was to wait for further information, and hope that most of the crew had remained aboard the ship.

After the electricity failed on board the *Notts County*, wireless operator Aabert had connected the batteries to the communications equipment. He tried to maintain constant contact with nearby vessels.

Two hours had passed since Robert Bowie jumped over-board from the *Notts County*. His shipmates had continued their attempts to puncture the raft, so that they could lift him back on board. Suddenly a huge wave washed the life raft over the ice-sheathed bulwarks and onto the deck under the boat-deck cas-ing where the men were standing. It was so long since they had last heard the shipmate's cries that they were convinced he must be dead.

Dick gazed blindly at the life raft that lay at his feet:

"We knew Robert was still in the life raft, but none of us dared open it. There was no chance he could still be alive. He must be dead. It was partly our fault that our shipmate lay frozen to death in the life raft—we hadn't managed to pull him back aboard while he was still alive.

None of us could even think of turning the raft over or open-ing the flaps and seeing what Robert looked like. We were all paralyzed with horror and fear.

'He's dead,' we all thought. We stood there in the storm, in awkward silence. Nobody said a word. We knew there was no chance the man could be alive after two hours in such a cold sea.

I was overcome with gruesome thoughts. I couldn't bear to imagine Robert, frozen, motionless—dead. I felt that my ship-mates were thinking the same. I had no idea whether we were going to get through this trial alive. If I looked into his face, I might be seeing myself as I would soon be. I'm sure I was not the only one thinking those thoughts as we stood there, exhausted and fearful.

None of us wanted to touch Robert Bowie. Nobody wanted to look at him. We were too scared even to approach the dead man.

We left the life raft lying on the deck. That struggle was over."

At half-past one, a signal from the trawler *Kingston Andalusite* had a chilling effect on the crew of the *Odin*. It was only now that they learned that the *Ross Cleveland* had been lost. Valdimar listened to the radio operator on the *Kingston Andalusite*:

"We believe the *Ross Cleveland* sank shortly before midnight. We were close to the trawler when she went down. We did not see anyone abandon ship."

The message was immediately relayed by the *Odin* to Isafjord. A search was organized at once, from Isafjord into the adjacent fjords. It had not been possible to contact rescue workers in the area. From Isafjord, notification was received that a search would be made from Bolungarvik at the Oshlid headland.

When Skipper Sigurdur heard the message, he grew thoughtful:

"When we received notification that the *Ross Cleveland* had gone down, I thought there was no hope of any survivors. The liferafts couldn't have withstood the storm. They would be bowled along like balls and blown away by the gale. As a rule the flaps give way first, and I thought that must have happened in that weather. It seemed incredible to me that a ship of six or seven hundred tons could sink in Isafjord Bay due to weather—in a place where ships commonly sought shelter. I was working on my own experience. Before that, I would have said that such a thing couldn't happen. I could hardly believe it. We thought the *Heidrun* had gone west of Bjarnarnupur, and taken shelter under Grænahlid."

Aboard the *Notts County*, the men were gathering on the bridge, where they felt safest. The skipper tried to reassure them. The hum of the communications equipment made them feel more secure—they were still in touch with nearby vessels. In addition, the bridge was well above the level of the deck, which was now being washed by the waves.

* * *

Petrified, Dick sat on a bench aft of the bridge:

"The three hours since we ran aground had passed in a flash. Aboard the ship, turmoil and panic had reigned. We knew our wireless operator had been sending out distress signals, and now I watched as he tried to contact other trawlers around us. He was constantly sending out: Mayday, Mayday, Mayday.

Skipper Burres did all he could to combat our fear and desperation. The engineers had their hands full keeping the emergency lights working, so we could see what we were doing. But the lights failed from time to time.

We had tried, in vain, to save the life of our shipmate.

And what followed was no better—just waiting. It was even worse. I had lost all hope. I was getting ready to die.

There was no heat aboard. Some of the men considered jumping overboard, trying to get to land, and walk ashore. But that was hopeless. Ashore, it was dark, a blizzard was blowing, and probably that bit of coast was uninhabited. Or maybe we hadn't run aground on the mainland at all, but on a skerry or deserted island? Then we would be no better off; wet, cold, and quite helpless. I had no idea where we were. And I was sure that, if we jumped overboard, we'd be swept away by the waves and smashed on the rocks before we could get anywhere.

The chances of reaching land alive by jumping overboard, and swimming against the wind in that hellish weather, were almost non-existent.

The skipper said it was best for us to stay on the bridge. We'd have to wait and see what happened. We had no option."

Some hours had passed since the *Ross Cleveland* foundered. In their life raft, Harry, boatswain Wally and sparehand Barry had suffered a horrible ordeal. One of the flaps of the raft was torn, and the other would not close properly.

Barry was wearing only his vest and pants. The youngest of the three, he had been at sea for two years, since he was sixteen. The lad had bailed alongside his shipmates in the life raft. He must have known what fate awaited him. Harry tried to keep them talking:

"I talked to him of my wife and my daughter. Barry told me of his boyhood in Hull, of his family and his mother. He looked weaker and weaker. Then he started to mutter and lay down in the bottom of the raft. I kept rubbing his hands and face to try and keep him alive. But it was no good."

Before the young man died, he had been seized with shuddering, then curled up, and lost consciousness.

Harry rubbed his hands and feet to stay warm. Wally kept bailing. There were now only 10 centimetres of water in the bottom of the raft, after his unceasing efforts. Wally, a father of four, was at the end of his strength. When he spoke, his speech was slurred and incoherent. Harry tried to cheer him up:

"I kept talking to him about his wife and his children. 'Hang on, Wally, hang on. There are ships around us and eventually they'll find us.' Oh God, we were so lonely out there."

Of all the crew of the *Ross Cleveland*, only Harry and Wally remained alive. Twelve of the crew had been family men, among them Fred Sawton, a fifty-year-old deckhand. His five children lost their father that night.

Aboard the life raft, there had not been much talk in the dark. Inadequately dressed, Wally was chilled to the bone. Harry had lost all sense of time. He had been calling out to Wally in the dark, but Wally stopped answering, and Harry soon realized he had lost consciousness. Harry was convinced that he too would die. His only consolation was that the life raft would not be swept out to sea, so their bodies would probably be found where the life raft was washed ashore, somewhere in Isafjord Bay.

Dick Moore noticed that the *Notts County* was now motionless:

"The sea no longer affected our balance, as the ship had settled down on the rocks. The eerie cracking, groaning noises we heard after the ship ran aground had ceased.

I sat on the bridge, listening to the howling storm. I felt the ship shaking at the mercy of the elements. We tried to keep warm on the bridge. It was icy-cold, and we were very uncomfortable. When we exhaled, you could see the steam of our breath against the faint battery-powered lights on the bridge.

Some of the men had wrapped themselves in blankets. I tried to listen when the radio operator made contact with other ships. First mate Stokes and Captain Burres were constantly trying to cheer us up. Stokes was limping—he had injured his leg trying to get the life raft aboard after a large lump of ice had fallen off the superstructure and hit him. Both the officers were suffering from the cold, especially their hands.

That night I left the bridge several times to go down to my cabin. It was so dark down there that you couldn't see your hand in front of your face. But I wanted to go down there and be alone.

'Is there any way to save any of my things?' I thought, but then realized that was a stupid idea. I would be lucky if I got away with my life, let alone any material objects. But the few things I owned, all my worldly goods, were there with me—like the only photos I had of my mother, who had died a few years before. I'd taken all my possessions with me from the room in Cleethorpes. Everything had gone into my sea bag.

I felt my way down the dark companionway in the cold. I felt I had to be alone—at least for a while. I wasn't a religious man, I'll freely admit. But I felt a need to pray.

Now I had faith.

My passport was in my cabin, and the silver-plated Parker pen that had great sentimental value to me, as it was the only thing I had left from my mother. She had given it to me on my nineteenth birthday. She died later that same year.

I clasped my hands and prayed. Now I was alone. But I felt I was too young to die. Only 25. My life was just beginning. I talked to God in heaven, and prayed to him to save me.

I thought of my girlfriend in Norway, my two sisters at home in Brighton, and my father. 'Will I never see my family again? Will I go the same way as Robert Bowie?'

And in my mind I heard his cries again, as he was tossed about helplessly in the icy sea. Again and again. And we, his ship-mates, could do nothing to save him.

That awful experience cut me to the heart.

When I got back to the bridge, I looked around at my ship-mates. They leaned against one another for warmth and comfort. I noticed that I was not the only one sneaking below—probably they had the same purpose in mind as I did, to be alone and pray. Now, when all we could do was pray, they were thinking of their loved ones."

John Davidson, a 23-year-old deckhand, had not been a church-going man, nor at all religious. But he, like Dick, had gone down to his cabin and prayed. He clasped his chilled hands. For a while he had been working with his bare hands to knock the ice off the ship:

"Dear God, let us get home safe!" John, like others, was thinking of his nearest and dearest.

If the crew of the *Notts County* thought their situation was hopeless, Harry Eddom's position was far worse, soaked to the skin in a life raft on the rough seas of Isafjord Bay.

He thought of Rita and Natalee at home, not knowing whether he would ever see them again. Was he going to die? Just when things were going so well for the family. In September they had bought a house in Cottingham, on the outskirts of Hull, with a garden for Natalee to play in. And Harry had planned to be home in the summer, when his little girl took her first steps. But now, he thought, his daughter would never see her Dad again. She would not even remember him.

The coastguard crew were convinced that nothing could be done for the grounded *Notts County* in the present weather conditions. They decided to try to locate the *Heidrun II*, and attempt to find better shelter, where it would be possible to clear the ice off the lower radar scanner.

Crewman Torfi Geirmundsson was on watch, with first mate Palmi:

"I was on the four-to-eight watch with Palmi. During the night I was sent up with him, in that wild weather, to help him with the ice. I wasn't much help. The conditions were so appalling that I mainly just clung onto the mast. Once Palmi slipped on the ladder, and hung on by one hand.

After that he told me to go down ahead of him, and take shelter. I had no option but to do as he said. With difficulty I managed to get down to the bridge wing and into the bridge. Skipper Sigurdur told me off for leaving Palmi. For a while it seemed that Palmi wasn't coming back. But after a while he came down from the bridge roof, with an injury to his hand.

I had to admire Palmi's stamina. It was all I could do up there just to cling on."

It was nearly 6 a.m. on Monday. Radio operator Valdimar heard the radio:

"*Odin, Odin*, Isafjord Radio calling!"

"Yes, Isafjord, I can hear you," Valdimar replied.

Barry Rogers, who died in the life raft from the Ross Cleveland.
❏ Dark Winter—The Hull Daily Mail

The Ross Cleveland—*starboard side. Harry Eddom managed to escape from the bridge as the vessel lay over on her side.*

The message from Isafjord was that a weak Mayday message had been heard from the *Notts County* around 5 a.m. They had made several attempts at replying, but it appeared that the trawler could not hear them.

The search for the *Heidrun* had yielded no result.

The weather was slightly improved below Grænahlid, and to the west beneath Bjarnarnupur. But all communications remained very difficult—even when the coastguard vessel was alongside another ship, they could hear little or nothing over the radio.

Dick was sitting on the bridge of the *Notts County*. The damp, freezing air was saturated with smoke and the sour fishy stink of the men's clothes. Dick's underclothes had become wet in the struggle to lift Robert Bowie back aboard; his damp clothes stuck to his chilled body. Dick shivered as he thought of the body of his shipmate lying on the deck below:

"The skipper was always trying his best to keep our spirits up. 'They'll come and rescue us. Don't worry, it will be all right,' he said, and poured out small glasses of rum that we passed around. We all got a little tot, but not too much. The idea was to warm us up, and cheer us up a little.

But we were all scared stiff.

When you looked out of the ice-sheathed windows, there was nothing outside but darkness.

Although we were given a sip of rum, we weren't supposed to be getting drunk. It wasn't possible to make any more tea—at least, no one was prepared to go down to the dark mess and galley and try.

It seemed to me that everyone expected us to die. And we hadn't heard that anyone was planning to rescue us."

The life raft off the *Ross Cleveland* was probably the only vessel on Isafjord Bay that nobody expected to be afloat.

Wally was now dead of exposure, frozen stiff in the ice-cold water in the bottom of the boat. Only Harry remained alive in the dark:

"I was lucky that I was fully rigged. I was wearing thick trousers, warm underclothing and a woollen jersey under a rubber duck suit and Wellington boots. I was dressed like that because I was on watch at the time." And the two young men who had saved his life were now dead of exposure. Harry was sure it was only a matter of time before he too died.

"But then I thought of everything I could to stop myself going to pieces. I thought of my wife at home. I thought about our baby Natalee."

Harry felt he was letting down his wife and daughter by dying—Harry the family man, who preferred to stay home on the rare occasions when he had the chance. He had spent little time down at the pub, compared with many others. He thought of the times when he invited his shipboard friends home for a beer. And he and Rita also saw their mothers regularly. Those times passed through his mind.

Meanwhile Rita slept with Natalee by her side in her warm bed at home in Cottingham—the woman who clung so faithfully to the seaman's life that she would not even go to the cinema when Harry was at sea.

News of the trawler's fate would soon be reaching Britain. He thought sadly of the knock at the door of his and Rita's home, and Rita learning of his death.

He had lost all hope as he curled up in the bottom of the life raft, doing his best to combat the painful cold:

"Barry had died after a few hours. I don't know how long. Wally died a bit later. I lost track of time. I just huddled in the bottom of the raft and wondered how long it was going to be before I followed them. I remember the wind was pushing us down the fjord. Day and night seemed to come and go."

Harry knew that the West Fjords were very sparsely populated, and he thought of their bodies being washed ashore in the life raft in some deserted place, never to be found.

It was nearly 8 a.m. and Harry was exhausted, his senses dulled with the cold. It was about nine hours since he had been plunged into the icy waters of Isafjord Bay.

Sigurdur Arnason had decided to sail the *Odin* back to the grounded *Notts County*. Radio operator Aabert aboard the *Notts County* was still transmitting Mayday, Mayday, Mayday. He kept going, hoping that the call might be heard.

It was heard by Valdimar aboard the *Odin*. This was the first direct contact with the grounded trawler. Valdimar also heard the British radio operator sending information that the crew were in poor condition.

The captain had noticed that morning that the winds were far higher under Bjarnarnupur than at the west of Isafjord Bay. Northeasterly force eight. As the coastguard vessel approached the grounded trawler, it was clear that they had no hope of spotting the vessel except on radar.

Valdimar soon made contact with the *Notts County*. "We're all on board," said Aabert in reply to Valdimar's enquiry. "And we have one life raft."

Valdimar replied at once. "We're one nautical mile from you. We'll do everything in our power to rescue you, but we have to wait for the weather to die down. Remain on board. Contact us again at ten o'clock."

A little more than half an hour after Valdimar's exchange with the *Notts County*, he thought he heard a garbled message from the *Notts County*'s radio operator on the microwave frequency. He thought he heard him say that a life raft from the vessel was about one nautical mile off shore—and that members of the crew were aboard. Another life raft had gone ashore!

Aboard the *Odin*, all hell broke loose. "Have the Englishmen gone mad? Don't they know they haven't a chance?" thought the coastguards.

Valdimar did all he could to establish better contact with the *Notts County*. He also raised the trawler *Prince Philip*, and informed her that the *Odin* was searching for a life raft from the *Notts County*, about a nautical mile offshore.

A few minutes later, Valdimar re-established contact with the radio operator of the grounded trawler.

"No, no, it's a misunderstanding about the life rafts," said Aabert when Valdimar asked him what was going on. "We're still all on board, but we're in a bad state," the radio operator said with emphasis.

The coastguard crew were relieved. "We'll do our best to rescue you. But stay aboard and wait. We'll be there as soon as we are able," said Valdimar.

The Icelandic radio operator was worn out. But the nervous tension of knowing of so many people in peril kept his attention fully on his work:

"The atmosphere on board was the way it often is when there's been an accident or there's a risk of something happening. The men did their jobs without comment. At sea, everyone knows what his own responsibilities are and there is no need to discuss it. You decide what needs to be done and do it. But if you did everything by the book you wouldn't get far.

I was sure we could send some men over to the trawler. But as to when, I didn't know. All I could do was to make sure the men kept going.

The radio operator had told me the *Notts County*'s batteries were running low.

I had urged them to stay on board. We knew from experience that a ship in that situation doesn't go anywhere. The northeasterly gale was blowing offshore, and wasn't doing any harm. The nearest building on shore was a summer cabin about two kilometres inland. The Englishmen had no hope of getting there in the dark and snow. I did my best to keep their hopes up."

* * *

On the radio, Icelanders were hearing of the events on Isafjord Bay. A storm had raged over much of the country during the night. Gudmundur Gudmundsson in Isafjord was so overwhelmed by the events of the night that he felt they could hardly be happening. Nothing had been heard of the *Heidrun II*.

In spite of the freak storm, Gudmundur found it hard to believe that a trawler of nearly 700 tons could go down almost within a stone's throw of the town of Isafjord itself.

"It seemed completely inconceivable. I had no idea whether anyone could have survived off the *Ross Cleveland*. We didn't know then how sudden it had been, or what the situation had been aboard. We had nothing to go on during the night.

I felt we were so helpless ashore. We couldn't do anything to help until the storm died down. We knew that if anyone had got into a life raft he would drift towards Alftafjord or Seydisfjord. You don't drift any complicated routes in weather like that."

As day dawned, Dick and his shipmates aboard the *Notts County* found they could discern the shoreline. The storm was still screeching, but the wind had dropped a little. There was snow all around:

"What I could see of the ship looked like a mound of snow and ice. We started talking about the chances of getting ashore. The coast was so close, and we felt very unsafe in the damaged ship. 'How can we get ashore?' asked the men. And if we got ashore, how deep was the snow, and which way should we go? There was no one there. We felt we were in the middle of no man's land.

Should someone swim ashore with a rope?

The suggestions weren't very sensible. The sea was too cold, the waves were too hazardous, and the weather was too

73

bad. 'We'll have to wait and see, at least until evening,' said the first mate. 'If no one's come to rescue us by them, we may have to do something ourselves, especially if the ship starts falling apart.'

I heard my mates saying that Aabert had apparently been in touch with Icelandic rescuers. He'd been told they couldn't reach us until daylight, and until the wind died down. I understood that—we were well aware how merciless the storm was."

Shortly afterwards, Valdimar's attention was caught. Something had happened aboard the *Notts County*.

The men felt a shiver down the spine when they heard:

"The hull's caved in. We're awash!"

The *Odin's* crew asked the British trawlermen to listen for the coastguard vessel's siren. Shortly afterwards they heard:

"We hear your siren!"

Now they had the first clear evidence that the *Odin* was in the right place. Valdimar assured the men once again that the coastguard crew would do all in their power to save them. A boat would be launched as soon as the weather permitted.

Valdimar also gave them the location of the coastguard vessel.

"We are half a nautical mile offshore. We'll stay here."

At about ten o'clock the *Notts County* announced that the ship was still aground and surrounded by water, the decks were awash but the crew of eighteen were all on the bridge, cold but dry. One man was dead from hypothermia and four had severe frostbite. One of the life rafts was still attached to the ship but was not accessible. The radio operator also said the tide had gone out and the ship had settled solidly on the rocks about a hundred metres from the shore.

By morning the weather in Isafjord Bay was dying down, but not on Snæfjallaströnd where the ship had run aground. The coastguard vessel tried sailing as close inshore as the depth of the water would permit. The knew they would have to take care not to run aground too. But in the poor visibility the Icelanders could not spot the trawler.

Valdimar was sending out a Morse message, reporting conditions in Isafjord Bay to the headquarters of the Iceland Coastguard:

"'Located at the point where the *Notts County* has run aground at Snæfjallaströnd, seven-and-a-half miles off Ædey island. Crew are still aboard. *Heidrun II* is missing. *Ross Cleveland* sank with all hands about 22:40 yesterday evening. At the place where the *Notts County* is grounded, wind speed is now north-northeast force ten, lower off the coast.'

It was incredible. A 700-ton ship had gone down almost next to us, another had run aground, and a boat was missing. It had all happened just outside the town of Isafjord. It was unreal."

Skipper Sigurdur was growing impatient, hoping that they could rescue the stranded men as soon as possible:

"We sent constant messages to the men on the *Notts County*, to keep waiting, to stay where they were. One of the other British trawlers had also been passing on messages.

Valdimar had been in the radio cabin the whole time, while I concentrated on navigating the ship. I wasn't constantly observing what went on in Valdimar's cabin, but I heard the buzz of the radio, and voices shouting.

When we opened a window to try to look out into the dark, against the snowstorm, you could hardly keep your eyes open."

* * *

Aboard the *Odin*, the men were trying to start a covered motor boat. The storm was abating a little. Valdimar sent another message to the coastguard headquarters:

"We are preparing for rescue—both fore scanners are damaged and two aerial masts broken, VHF radio aerial damaged by the storm."

This did not mean, however, that it was regarded as safe to set off from the coastguard vessel in that small boat. The *Notts County* reported that five men now had frostbite and another two were ill. At this point the radio operators of the coastguard vessel and the trawler were in near-constant contact. What the British radio operator wanted to know was:

"When are you coming?"

Valdimar did all he could to calm the crew of the *Notts County*:

"We'll be there soon. I'm sure you will be rescued."

He felt sorry for the radio operator:

"I heard sadness, even fear, in his voice. I assumed that most of the crew were on the bridge, very close to him, listening to everything we said over the radio. Under the circumstances, he was amazingly self-possessed, after all that had happened.

He kept asking when we were coming.

He was still transmitting using batteries. I was astonished at how long they lasted."

Harry Eddom lay, cold and sodden, curled up in the bottom of the *Ross Cleveland*'s life raft. About twelve hours had passed since the trawler went down:

"As dawn was breaking the raft crunched onto some rocks at the end of the fjord. I staggered out, managed to pull the raft up a bit, and wandered up the valley. I knew if I stopped I wouldn't get anywhere."

Harry had no idea where he was. The raft had washed ashore on a stretch of coast beneath some cliffs. He knew he must be on the south side of Isafjord Bay. He knew the fjords were sparsely populated, and in the poor visibility of the storm it was difficult to see anything.

He spotted lights on the other side of the fjord—miles away. He knew his chance of reaching safety was minimal, but he set off all the same, pausing only to try to wring out his sopping-wet socks. He sat down and tugged one boot off, and with difficulty managed to wring out the sock with his numb hands. He abandoned the idea of taking off the other boot—it was just too difficult and painful.

Captain Sigurdur was starting to see the real possibility of starting the rescue operation:

"All morning we'd been trying to start the engine of the covered boat. But it was impossible to start the air-cooled diesel engine in that cold. I felt the risk would be far less if we could send the men over in the covered boat.

Just after midday, I discussed with Sigurjon whether we might send an inflatable boat over to the trawler to rescue the crew. Sigurjon volunteered to go, along with Palmi and third mate Sigurjon Ingi. I decided to send Sigurjon and Palmi."

Sigurjon, like Palmi, was experienced with small boats in rough seas. He was starting to plan the rescue:

"Since we couldn't start the engine of the big diesel-powered boat, the only option was to take the Zodiac, which had a good Johnson outboard motor, nine-and-a-half horsepower. Those motors were easy to handle, and well-shielded. Even if the sea washed over them they kept running, and they were very reliable if properly treated.

Palmi was not the only volunteer. One of the others was third mate Sigurjon Ingi. To my mind, it wasn't a question of whether or not you dared to go—we simply had to go and rescue those men. It was a task that had to be done."

The crew of the *Odin* worked all for one. Chief engineer Larus Magnusson had assigned engineers to both engines. And the crew thought of Skipper Sigurdur, who would now attempt to sail the *Odin* as close inshore as he could, almost up onto the shore. Sigurjon and Palmi boarded the Zodiac as it hung from a derrick with the motor running. The boat was lowered over the rail and out over the side. Now they waited for the opportunity to launch the boat at the skipper's signal.

Valdimar was on the bridge with Sigurdur:

"Once Sigurjon and Palmi started getting ready, I was rushing back and forth between the radio cabin and the bridge. Sigurdur was out on the bridge wing, and wanted me to monitor the depth sounder and keep him informed of the depth of the water, while others kept an eye on the radar screen.

Sigurdur did not want Sigurjon and Palmi to leave until they had a sighting of the trawler. He urged the ship on, foot by foot. He told Sigurjon to monitor the radar screen, and me to read off the depth sounder.

Once Sigurdur called out: 'What's the depth?'

'Zero,' I replied. The ship was almost running aground."

Sigurdur remained calm:

"Suddenly Valdimar called out that the depth sounder wasn't showing anything—in other words, there was no water under the ship. I just said 'all right.' I fully expected the *Odin* to touch bottom.

'Hell,' I cursed under my breath. 'If there was ever a time to take a risk, this is it. That's what coastguard vessels are for.' We just had to hope that it would be all right.

The crew of the Odin *finally caught sight of the stranded* Notts County *through the blizzard. It was time for action.*
❑ Valdimar Jonsson

Now the distance between the *Notts County* and us was 0.1 nautical mile—under 200 metres. We could just make out the shape of the trawler, on the shore. The snow was pelting down, a northeasterly gale blowing at force eight to nine, and there were quite choppy waves, as the wind was blowing at an angle off-shore.

When I had gone as far as I dared, I turned the *Odin* around against the wind, providing some shelter on the starboard side, where the men were waiting to launch the boat with Sigurjon and Palmi aboard."

Palmi was ready for anything. He too had spotted the *Notts County*:

"I was delighted to see that the ship was actually there. We'd heard that all the crew were on the bridge. Suddenly it no longer seemed an impossible task to rescue them.

But we had to take care.

The Zodiac was hanging out over the side, and Sigurjon and I were ready. The boat was lowered, and the motor was running. We were ready to go.

Since the wind was blowing at an angle off the shore, the waves didn't wash over the trawler. But the build-up of ice was extraordinary. I realized that if the ship hadn't run aground there, it would have capsized out on the fjord, and the men would have been lost, as on the *Ross Cleveland*. That ship had lost all stability. It couldn't have remained afloat another hour.

The crew had abandoned the attempt to get rid of the ice. It was their good fortune to run aground."

Sigurjon sat by the motor in the stern of the boat:

"We were hardly more than 200 metres from the *Notts County*. We knew that the weather was much better off the shore than there, under Snæfjallaströnd. The wind was funnelling down past the mountain, causing eddies.

We took two uninflated rubber life-rafts with us as ballast in the Zodiac; they were spare rafts, packed in sailcloth. We also took them along because we didn't know if we might need them for the rescue.

The major risk was that the boat might capsize under us in the eddies, or run aground in the shallows."

The skipper watched Palmi and Sigurjon go. There was tension in the air:

"Now all we could do was wait, and hope that the two mates would be successful. The wind was carrying us farther out. We'd decided that the lads would take a walkie-talkie with them, so we could maintain contact. I'd ordered them, if they managed to rescue the men, not to leave the trawler without letting us know. Then I would slowly move close inshore, as far in as I dared, until they saw us and could set off.

We thought it was safer for them to take the rubber dinghies; it was well known that if those Zodiac boats were not handled right in high winds they sometimes capsized.

We were apprehensive of that. But I knew Palmi was lying in the bow to weight it down, while Sigurjon was sitting at the windward side, steering the boat."

It was one-thirty. Fourteen hours had passed since the *Notts County* ran aground. The men aboard were nervous wrecks. News of the events on Isafjord Bay had now reached Britain. Rita, like other family members of the *Ross Cleveland*'s crew, was being informed that the trawler had capsized, and that there was little hope of any survivors. Those who heard the news, especially seamen's families who were familiar with conditions off Iceland, knew that no one could live for long after immersion in the sea. Harry Eddom's father, also named Harry, had himself been a fisherman in Icelandic waters. He told his wife Minnie, Harry's mother, that he did not believe anyone could have survived.

Valdimar was sending a message to the *Notts County*—the message they had long been waiting for:
"Our boat is on its way over to you!"

Palmi lay on top of the life rafts in the Zodiac, to prevent the wind sweeping under the bow and flipping the boat over:
"The wind that was blowing against the boat was enormously strong. The trawler was in sight, but I saw that we were losing sight of the *Odin*.
I'd decided to wear a wetsuit. Over it I wore a duck suit, against the wind-chill. Wetsuits are particularly bad in windy conditions, when you chill quickly. But if you've got something to prevent the chilling, you can stay quite warm. So I thought I would be all right if I found myself in the sea.
Sigurjon, on the other hand, was wearing long underwear, warm trousers and a thick anorak. Nothing could be allowed to go wrong, because if our boat capsized and we found ourselves in

the icy-cold sea, we could forget about collecting our old-age pensions. On the other hand, we were wearing life vests, so at least we wouldn't sink."

Sigurjon peered into the blizzard:

"As soon as I saw a squall coming, I released the clutch to reduce speed, and Palmi and I pushed down the windward side. We hung over the side by sitting astride the gunwale, which was rounded, with our heads down. We had to take care not to be pulled under the boat if she capsized. The main risk was that the wind might catch the front of the boat and lift it up—since most of the weight was in the stern.

After the squall had passed over, I re-engaged the clutch, and we went on.

I always saw the squalls as they approached. They were whirlwinds, really. Palmi and I could always see what was happening, so we didn't have to call out to each other."

The young crewman on the *Odin*, Torfi, was apprehensive:

"When I saw Palmi and Sigurjon vanish into the snow and the darkness, I never expected to see them again. The conditions there were too dangerous for such a small boat—in that violent storm. They'd volunteered to go out into danger in a rubber dinghy.

I was horrified that they had decided to do it. I'd always looked up to Palmi and Sigurjon, and been proud of them. But only a few seconds after they set off from the coastguard ship, they had vanished. I never thought I'd see them again."

Palmi was far from happy at the way the squalls tugged at the boat:

"On the way over, I felt that the boat was on the point of being flipped by the wind. I didn't like the look of it. The slightest thing could capsize the boat. Then we'd be flung into the sea, the motor would stall, and we wouldn't be able to start it again. And the *Odin* was drifting farther and farther away from us, so our shipmates would have no hope of finding us. And our walkie-talkie would get wet, so we wouldn't be able to let anyone know where we were.

We'd have no chance at all in that cockleshell. Just one wave would have done for us.

During our years at sea, Sigurjon and I had both had boats capsize under us in heavy seas. When that happens, the golden rule is to keep hold of the boat. You can try to use the outboard motor as a step, to climb up onto the keel. But then you soon get exhausted. I felt that, since I was wearing a wetsuit, I might be able to use the wind to help me right the boat."

Sigurjon was also considering their situation:

"I was wearing a sheepskin anorak. Under my clothes I had long woollen underwear, as you always do in such weather conditions. I was also wearing waders, a balaclava helmet, and woollen gloves, of course.

Palmi and I were both qualified divers, but he had thought ahead, and decided to wear a wetsuit, with a duck suit over it, so he wouldn't get wet. But I don't know that either of us would have been up to much, if we'd finished up in the sea. I hadn't given myself time to think about all that before we set off. Nobody could have performed any great feats in that situation, if the boat had capsized. We'd simply have had to hang onto the boat.

I had to admire our boat's motor—simply the way it kept running! We had the same problems on that little boat as on the *Odin*—the same frost and icing. Ice piled up on the boat, including the motor and the crew—that is, Palmi and me. We were encrusted with ice, the motor housing was sheathed in ice—the freezing-cold sea water washed over everything, freezing solid as soon as it hit.

But we had no time to worry about that. We were on our way over to the trawler to rescue the crew. It remained to be seen whether we would succeed.

We moved slowly on."

Dick Moore knew that something important was happening.

"The radio operator had told us that a ship was coming. That gave us hope of rescue. Shortly afterwards someone called out:

'There's a ship astern of us!'

I turned, and saw the outline of a ship—it was a coastguard vessel. What a beautiful sight! Then the ship vanished, and we glimpsed a small rubber dinghy. I didn't like the look of that. We couldn't all fit into that little boat.

Captain Burres and the radio operator were talking to the coastguard vessel on the radio. The men started going outside, and gathering on the bridge wing."

The ship's cook, 52-year-old Harry Sharpe from Grimsby, had been sure until that moment that he was going to die. His son had been lost at sea eight years before.

As he watched Palmi and Sigurjon approach, he realized that the two Icelanders were risking their lives for him and his shipmates—their inflatable boat might capsize at any moment. Harry knew that if those men succeeded in saving his life he would be eternally grateful to them. "We're freezing to death here, and those men are our only hope," he thought, like the others on board.

When Frank McGuinness, a 30-year-old deckhand who had been fishing off Iceland for years, looked out at the ship, he thought to himself that he would never have believed that he could be so delighted at the sight of an Iceland Coastguard ship approaching!

Sigurjon was considering the best way to come up to the grounded ship:

"Soon we approached the trawler. The surf had washed her ashore at high tide, but now the tide was out. The *Notts County* was stuck fast, but had settled down so there was a lot of water in the hold and engine room. The sea was almost up to the deck, but the superstructure was well above the water level, so probably everything in there was dry.

Part of the trawl was hanging down from the ice on the starboard side. We saw a capsized life raft still attached to the stern of the ship. We were coming up alongside the *Notts County*."

Aboard the *Odin*, the men were thoughtful, not least Torfi Geirmundsson:

"The men were alarmed, especially the younger ones, like me. We realised how serious the situation was, and we knew that Palmi's and Sigurjon's expedition could end in tragedy. We did our best to conceal our anxiety and think of other things. One of us was always joking. But even he didn't say a word, for once.

All we could do was carry on hacking the ice off the ship, try to keep the *Odin*, which was listing badly, on an even keel, and hope for the best."

Dick Moore said a little prayer of thanks when he saw the coastguards on their way over—not least because he, like the rest of the crew, had fully expected to die. Now it looked as if there was some hope of being rescued. Or was there?

Suddenly it appeared to Dick that the Icelandic boat was veering away from the trawler. Something was up.

* * *

Sigurjon did not like what he saw as he and Palmi drew close to the trawler.

"I looked up, towards the bridge. I suddenly saw a crowd of men come bursting out of the bridge. They lined up down the bridge wing, and over to the superstructure, to come down the gangway. At least two of them were waving bottles of liquor. It seemed as though they wanted to offer us a drink!

I didn't like the look of that.

We had to get the men off and back to our ship as quickly as possible, because the weather was very bad and conditions hazardous. As I looked at the crowd of men, I tried to spot if any of them were drunk. If so, they would be a danger, as they would be less likely to follow our instructions.

'They're drunk,' I thought.

There was no way I dared tie up to the trawler until we were sure it was safe to come alongside. If we sailed up to the ship immediately, the desperate men, who had been waiting for more than twelve hours to be rescued, might simply jump down into the boat.

It was a risk we couldn't take.

So I used my initiative, and employed some vocabulary I'd actually learned from the British years before.

I stopped the boat, disengaged the clutch, and let the boat drift away from the side of the vessel."

Sigurjon Hannesson, first mate of the *Odin*, prepared to give the British crew a talking-to. Coated in ice, he was a grotesque sight in his sheepskin anorak, his balaclava helmet encrusted in icicles. All that could be seen of Sigurjon's face were his dark, sharp eyes.

He stood up, raised one wader up on the gunwale, shook a fist and shouted out:

"'If you don't do as I say, you can go to Hell, and we'll go back to our ship!'

The crew fell silent, frozen where they were. Suddenly everything went quiet."

Sigurjon saw that his strategy was working:

"I saw that they all went quiet. They understood.

'And to Hell with your booze,' I shouted."

Dick was well aware that no one on board was drunk. He knew that the skipper, who was severely frostbitten and exhausted, was so grateful to the Icelanders for coming to their rescue that he wanted to give them the bottles of spirit that were left in the bond, as they would only have gone down with the ship.

"But the Icelanders made it very clear they didn't think that was appropriate. They were quite direct about it.

In the end I saw the skipper throw the bottle into the sea. There was no other choice.

The skipper told us all to stay calm. We would have to do exactly as they said. Not rush into anything. The atmosphere aboard was very tense. Finally someone had come to our rescue.

The Icelanders were extraordinarily cool-headed. They gave the orders now. I put on my still-wet jacket over my woolly jumper, then went outside and waited my turn to abandon ship."

Palmi had been as disquieted as Sigurjon when he saw men waving bottles of spirits under those circumstances:

"The English were known for giving out tots of rum or other spirits when some problem arose. In the past there had even been stories of Englishmen who were too drunk to get into the breeches-buoy when they were being rescued. So we weren't entirely surprised.

But then I saw that the men were simply terrified, not drunk at all. They'd seen the *Ross Cleveland* capsize and go down with all hands just a stone's throw from them. I gathered that the crew of the *Notts County* had been in contact with the crew of the *Ross Cleveland* until just seconds before they died.

I saw a capsized life raft tied up to a line on the starboard side. It was blowing about in the storm. Sigurjon and I managed to get hold of the raft and bale the water out of it—and make it ready to transport the crew.

The wind was howling, but at least we didn't have to cope with heavy surf, as the storm was blowing off-shore. The crew were lowering a rope ladder."

Eighteen men stood out in the storm, some poorly clad, on the deck of the *Notts County*. For most of the night and all morning they had been sitting on the bridge and in the radio cabin of the trawler. They now felt more optimistic about their chances of survival, but as soon as they emerged from the bridge they felt the fierce cold and the gale funnelling down off the ice-clad shore of Snæfjallaströnd.

Sigurjon was busy helping the men down:

"The crew were waiting up by the gunwale, and did just as we said. I'd been informed that there were eighteen of them. That meant we would have to use two rafts to transport them over to the *Odin*. We didn't want to have to make two trips.

Palmi and I tied up our boat to the trawl that was hanging down off the ice-sheathed side. We then set to work to right the life raft that had been floating upside-down tied to the trawler. We turned it over, and got most of the water out.

We decided to inflate one of our own rubber life rafts, and attach it by a rope line to the ship's life raft. That would give us two rafts for taking the men over to the coastguard vessel. To help the men into the rafts, Palmi and I could move over into the life raft, and stand at the flap opening. If we could keep one foot down inside the raft and the other on the gunwale, we could catch the men as they jumped down. We'd be like doormen."

Dick observed in admiration as the Icelanders worked down below:

"I decide to give way to the men who were in a worse condition than me. We formed a queue at the gunwale. There was no panic now—we knew it was best to follow the Icelanders' instructions. Skipper Burres had quite bad frostbite, especially his hands, and Stokes the mate had injured his leg.

The skipper had been with us when we were trying to save Robert Bowie and helped us try to get the life raft back on board. He hadn't been nearly as warmly dressed as the rest of us, who'd been out on deck clearing ice before we ran aground. He had been bare-handed, with neither a duck suit nor gloves—unlike us."

Sigurjon decided they were ready. He looked up to the men on board:

"We told the Englishmen what we wanted to do: 'You jump down, one at a time. Then each of you is to crawl through the raft we're in now, and into the other life raft. When there are nine men aboard, you close the flap. Then the other nine men can come down into this raft, and close the flaps when you're all aboard. Then we'll try to tow both rafts across to the ship.'

They didn't need telling twice. They nodded as they listened to our instructions.

They were ready.

I looked up again, and signalled that the first man could jump down. The reaction was quick. The first man climbed up onto the gunwale down the rope ladder, and jumped into the raft. Palmi and I each caught hold of one arm. He did as we had said—crawled through the life raft, and into the other one.

I noticed that the men who were most warmly dressed stood aside and waited, allowing the others to go ahead. It looked as if some of the crew were carrying bottles as they prepared to board the raft.

I told them, to Hell with your bottles. I didn't see any after that. They must have thrown them into the sea."

Palmi was now face to face with the Englishmen who had been waiting for twelve hours in peril, while the coastguards tried to come to their aid:

"They seemed to be in very variable condition. Some were just wearing a vest and a jacket. Others were wearing duck suits, and warmly-dressed. When they got down into the raft, we started to have problems getting them through the life raft into the other one. They wanted to hug us, they were so relieved.

We really had to pry them off, and shove them through the life raft."

Sigurjon noticed that one of the crew was very poorly dressed:

"One of them was wearing a suit and ordinary shoes. I thought he might be the radio operator. When he jumped down, unfortunately we didn't manage to catch him, and he fell down between the ship and the Zodiac. For some reason Palmi and I weren't quick enough. The man, who was wearing a life vest, was plunged up to his waist into the sea. To get him aboard, Palmi kept hold of him at the flap of the life raft, while I climbed over into the Zodiac. I knelt down by the gunwale, and got my arms under his life vest, so I could get hold of him by the waist. I pulled him up to my chest, then threw myself back into the boat. And that was how I got him aboard.

But he didn't move. I had to push him aside to get back to Palmi, and keep on helping the others aboard.

The poor man was exhausted, and motionless. I don't know if he was simply paralyzed with fear, but he did nothing to save himself. He had put all his faith in others. He knew, like the others aboard, that although we often challenged them for fishing in Icelandic waters, and although we weren't necessarily the best of friends, they could rely on the coastguard rescuing them if necessary. We were men, like them. When it was a question of life and death, nobody was thinking of politics, fishing limits or Cod Wars.

It was simply one seaman coming to the rescue of another."

The man who had plunged into the sea between ship and boat was radio operator Joyce Aabert. His duties rarely took him out on deck, so he was not warmly dressed. The next man was Dick. He scrambled over the icy bulwark, grabbed the rope ladder and jumped down to Palmi and Sigurjon:

"As I crawled into the first life raft, I felt immediately that I was on the sea again. I could feel the sharp, strong movement under the life raft. It was as if the waves were embracing the little boat. For hours we'd been on the motionless trawler, which had settled on the rocks. But now we could feel the elements once again.

I didn't feel particularly safe. We had got off the trawler, but now we were at the mercy of the waves—the same waves that had cost Robert Bowie his life. We were in precisely the same place as he had been, as he fought for his life. When the flaps of the life raft were closed, we could no longer see out. You somehow lost your sense of balance, and you could only feel the swell of the sea and the waves.

I felt sick.

Once again, I could sense the desperation of my shipmates. We were far from safe, although we were in the life raft."

Sigurjon was considering what to do about the radio operator:

"He lay there motionless on top of me in the Zodiac. I pushed him aside to get free. But when I stood up, he simply lay staring up.

He didn't move.

I couldn't hang about, so I went back to join Palmi. We had to get on with the job. I decided to leave the man where he was.

Once we had got everyone off the ship, he was still lying there motionless in the Zodiac. We had to get him out of the boat. We couldn't set off with him lying there on top of all the stuff—including the ropes we were going to use to tow the life rafts.

Palmi and I clambered over into the Zodiac, and picked up the unconscious man. His glasses had come off, and fallen down into the boat. He had made no attempt to keep hold of them.

We started off by putting his glasses back on. It was quite a job to get him over into the other raft. When we'd stood him up, and went to help him over into the life raft, we realized that the other men had conscientiously followed our instructions and closed the flap.

We told them to open it up again. 'Open up! Open up!' we shouted. We could hear turmoil inside, but nothing happened for a while. We wanted to be off back to the *Odin*. We felt they were far too slow in doing as we asked. By now there was a little gap, and we were getting annoyed at how long it was taking.

We decided not to mess about any more. Palmi and I picked the man up and shoved him unceremoniously in through the gap."

The mates now had only one life raft as ballast in the Zodiac on their way back to the ship, but now the wind was blowing from behind them, on the port side.

Palmi considered the conditions before setting off back to the Odin:

"We weren't supposed to set off until the *Odin* was back in sight. We were sure all the crew had left the ship—that and no one was left alive aboard. There were eighteen men in the two life rafts, and Sigurjon and I were in the Zodiac.

On the way back we wouldn't need as much ballast and extra weight as before. The three vessels, tied together, were like one big raft.

Sigurjon took out the walkie-talkie to call up the *Odin*.

"We're ready to go!" He shouted.

"Palmi and I had a rope aboard the Zodiac, which we had tied to the life raft off the *Notts County* that lay closest to the ship. We cut the rope that had attached us to the ship. At the back of our boat we tied a sort of harness so we could tow the life rafts.

Soon after we set off we spotted the *Odin*.

We sailed on slowly but surely. The men in the life rafts didn't make a sound. I could imagine them sitting inside there, motionless. We tried to go as slow as possible, to make sure the ropes would hold."

Now the captain of the *Odin* had to sail into the shallows again—risking the ship once more so that Palmi and Sigurjon would be able to see her. If they lost sight of her, they might be swept out into the fjord, with unforeseeable consequences. They had a walkie-talkie, but no equipment to tell them where they were. Although the coastguard vessel had radar, it would not be reliable for locating the small life rafts.

Boatswain Egill Palsson had been asked to have men ready to receive the Englishmen, and steward Haukur Jonsson had been instructed to prepare something hot, and plenty of blankets, for the rescued men.

Skipper Sigurdur moved the ship forward dead slow to the place where they had parted company with Sigurjon and Palmi. The skipper had been closely observing the trawler, which he could see on the radar screen as a small projection from the mainland.

"I knew that on my ship the transducer for the depth sounder was located fore. Valdimar was monitoring the depth sounder, and Sigurjon Ingi the radar. I was well aware we were taking a big risk.

I'm no different from anyone else when it comes to risks—you try to avoid them. But how can you avoid taking a risk when it's a matter of trying to save lives? I fully expected the *Odin* to touch bottom. Even if that happened, it would only dent the hull. Provided she was moving slowly, the damage would be minor. Even if we ran aground, the offshore wind would tend to push us off.

It was a certain consolation."

The *Odin* moved slowly inshore. The skipper's heart was racing. Everyone was on the lookout—where was the British trawler, and where were Sigurjon and Palmi? Sigurdur gave certain orders from the bridge, but the main thing was to spot the men. The ship crept forward, foot by foot.

"Are you on the depth finder, Valdimar? What's it reading now?" called the skipper, peering out into the blizzard.

"Two metres," called the radio operator, and, shortly afterwards, "One metre." And Sigurjon Ingi informed the captain that the grounded trawler was 0.1 nautical miles (185 metres) away.

Suddenly there was a shout: "There they are. They're there!" The snowstorm was easing slightly and visibility was getting a little better.

They could see the outlines of the trawler and the orange life rafts.

The mates aboard the Zodiac caught sight of the grey shape of the coastguard ship. Sigurjon set off.

Dick was apprehensive inside the closed life raft.

"Would our life raft capsize? Would we be fighting for our lives inside a closed life raft like Robert Bowie? And we were all crammed together. Would those two Icelanders have any hope of rescuing us if the life raft capsized? Bowie had been alone in the life raft the night before, while there were nine of us crowded together, and another nine in the other raft. I found the situation unsettling.

'Stay calm and sit still. Don't move around any more than you have to!' Stokes the mate called out. We could hear the Icelanders outside; they seemed very decisive.

I felt that the life raft was being tossed about on the waves. My heart was in my mouth as the raft lifted up suddenly, then dropped down again. It moved strangely and unpredictably—it was quite new to me, and I found myself feeling seasick. Other men were feeling the same way. We sat in a circle on the icy-cold bottom of the raft.

My main fear was that the raft might capsize. We held on to each other—I thought everyone felt the same. But the men talked quietly, not paying attention to each other. There was an overwhelming nervous tension in the air. We tried not to show how scared we were."

Sigurjon felt that conditions were quite different now from when he had sailed over to the trawler.

"Now the wind was mostly at our backs. It seemed to be going fine. We could see skipper Sigurdur was sailing toward us, as close as he could. I saw him steer the *Odin* incredibly close to the shore."

* * *

Torfi Geirmundsson had been watching, peering out into the storm to see if he could spot Sigurjon and Palmi again:

"As soon as I spotted the boat out in the snow, I was overcome with delight. I'd never expected the two mates to get back to us. I was just so pleased we'd got our companions back, and that we'd been able to take part in saving the British seamen.

Palmi and Sigurjon had done a brave deed."

Sigurjon was considering how best to tow the life rafts up alongside the *Odin*:

"When we were below the stern of the *Odin*, the skipper tried steering away from the shore to stop her running aground.

I noticed that my friend the engineer, Bjarni Gudbjörnsson, was at the gunwale—a big, strong man, with a firm, warm grasp. He and other members of the crew would lift the shipwrecked men aboard.

Palmi and I tried to hold the rafts steady while our shipmates helped the Englishmen board. When the *Odin* moved astern to get into deeper water, she turned into the wind, so it was awkward for us at the stern.

The ship was listing to starboard, and it looked as if the men could just step right up on deck—water was washing into the alleyway on the starboard side. It was because of both the icing and the storm blowing on the port side—although the wind had dropped a little. You could only imagine what it had been like at its worst."

Twenty-four coastguards were busy preparing to receive the eighteen shipwrecked trawlermen. Below decks they had blankets and quilts ready, along with warm clothes, soup, more food, tea and coffee. Everything was prepared for the exhausted, fearful guests.

The atmosphere was tense.

The coastguards knew their ship had sailed so close to the shore that it might quite probably touch bottom. The crew were nervous—exhausted, tense, yet above all pleased at their success as "fishers of men." This time they were not apprehending British seamen for fishing in Icelandic waters. The British ship had, admittedly, been well within the 12-mile limit, but that was not an issue now. Nobody had even thought of shooting a trawl in that weather.

But the eighteen men were a good "catch" for the coast-guard, all the same. As always when lives are saved, they were filled with a sense of satisfaction and pride. A unique pleasure.

Yet the fate of the *Heidrun* and the *Ross Cleveland*, and the man whom they had not been able to save off the *Notts County*, cast a shadow over them. The crew of the *Ross Cleveland* was believed lost, and there were fears for the *Heidrun II*, of which there had been no news for more than twelve hours.

Dick was looking forward to getting aboard the coastguard vessel. He was aware of someone catching hold of the flaps of the life raft, and starting to unfasten them. The Englishmen heard talk outside the raft, but since it was in Icelandic they understood nothing.

Dick peeked out through the gap. He saw the ice-laden coastguard vessel—a listing iceberg. On the boat deck were sturdy lifeboats. It seemed to him that the Icelandic crewmen held out innumerable helping hands.

Sigurjon was concentrating on holding the Zodiac and the two life rafts up close to the *Odin*:

"As the port side was the windward side, and the ship had sailed close inshore, she had to sail astern. So it was difficult for us to keep the life rafts up close to the door in the bulwark, while the Englishmen boarded. When the ship moved astern she turned into the wind, and the waves struck the Zodiac. But it went fine.

As soon as the skipper was far enough from land, and he could see that there was no longer any danger of the coastguard ship running aground, he let her drift, and we came around alongside again, and it went very well.

He did an excellent job."

Most of the crew of the *Notts County* were in a poor condition: cold, shivering, hungry, frostbitten, some injured. It was not far for them to go from the gunwale to the two messes on the starboard side. All the men had been through a terrifying ordeal, and were still in a state of shock. Dick was one of the few who had been fairly warmly dressed:

"We were helped aboard. In the mess we sat on benches at tables. One of the officers started making a note of our names. I took off my jacket—it was warm and comfortable in there. Not like the trawler we'd just left.

At last we were safe—probably few of us had believed we would ever reach safety. Most of us had expected to die.

"The officer who was taking the details of the survivors eventually reached me. I felt so grateful for the risks the crew of the *Odin* had taken to save our lives, that I wanted in some way to show my gratitude. But I felt that just saying 'thank you' was not good enough. I then remembered the Parker pen I had managed to salvage from my cabin, and thought, I could give this to the officer taking the names. I realised he would not know the significance of the pen to me, or how much I treasured it, but I would know, and would get a lot of satisfaction from that.

When the Icelander with the pen and the notebook asked me my name, I reached into my pocket for the pen my mother had given me just before she died. I don't know what the man's job on the ship was, nor his name. At first he would not take the pen.

But I said I wanted him to have the pen as a token of my gratitude for saving my life. He again refused, saying it was part of his job, and any seaman would have done the same, but I insisted, asking him to accept it. Eventually he seemed to take pity on me and reluctantly accepted the pen, thanking me for the gift. I'm sure the man had no need for a pen, but he accepted it, doing it to help me."

Sigurjon could breathe more easily now:

"The *Odin* was now headed for Isafjord. The life rafts were stowed. I decided to go down to the mess. The first thing I saw when I walked into the mess was a man sitting there bare-arsed. I recognised the man at once—he was the man in the suit that had fallen in the water when getting off the ship. It turned out that one of the crew had helped him out of his wet trousers, and he hadn't been wearing any underwear. He still had his jacket and shirt on. The poor man was so cold, and someone was trying to warm him up.

It was clear that five of the Englishmen had been fairly warmly dressed. They were fine. They'd been working out on deck—deckhands who were wearing good protective clothing, duck suits and sweaters. All of them could have survived for some time aboard the trawler. But I wouldn't have liked to bet that any of the rest of the crew could have made it through the night.

I thought it was strange they were all so cold, since we knew that most of the trawler had been above the water—probably the galley, the mess and the cabins amidships. I turned to one of the men and asked:

'Didn't you have any heating in the ship? Couldn't you have made a coal fire?'

'The engines were oil-fired,' he replied.

'But didn't you have other things you could have burned to make a fire? Benches and so on?'

The man simply shrugged.

I realized that probably the men had been reluctant to leave the bridge, and the safety of the group, while they were waiting."

Skipper Sigurdur handed over control to third mate Sigurjon Ingi, and settled down to debrief Palmi and Sigurjon. They told him the trip over to the *Notts County* had progressed slowly—as the wind had been gusting down off the mountains, making things difficult for them. The squalls had come close to capsizing the Zodiac. As the coastguard vessel sailed away from Snæfjallas-trönd, the men soon felt that the storm was abating a little. It had clearly been much worse where the *Notts County* ran aground.

Torfi Geirmundsson helped to take care of the ship-wrecked men:

"It was obvious the Englishmen were severely traumatized. I'd never seen that before. My job was to help the men into the mess. I noticed that as soon as I'd helped them to a seat, they simply sat staring into space. Our mess boys brought them hot drinks at once.

The fear in the men's faces was a saddening sight. I'd never seen a whole group of men shocked into numbness like that. There was hardly a man among them who could speak a word."

Valdimar was one of those who joined the rescued men in the mess:

"Skipper Sigurdur told me to go below, find the captain, and ask if all the crew were accounted for.

I went below to the mess. It was a miserable sight. One of the men had lost his boots and one sock. Another was in his vest, and a third had taken off his wet things and was half-naked. It was only then that I realized why they had been in such a hurry to be rescued. I was shocked at how poorly dressed they were.

The captain's hands were badly frost-bitten, but he seemed to be physically very fit. He told me that all the crew members who were still alive were now on board the *Odin*. I noticed that four or five of the crew seemed to be warmly dressed, in thick sweaters and boots. I knew that the British sometimes started drinking when there was trouble. Although they did not seem to be under the influence, I still thought a lot of them were in worse condition than they need have been."

The rescued men were given emergency medical attention, and the *Odin* contacted the regional hospital at Isafjord, as some of them had frostbite. The worst affected were Captain Burres and first mate Stokes. News of the rescue had reached Isafjord and elsewhere. Arrangements were made to contact the British consul, Brian Holt, in Reykjavik. Hannes Hafstein of the Life-Saving Association closely monitored events. Though from a distance, he supervised the search for the *Heidrun II*, and for the bodies of any men who might have been washed overboard from the *Ross Cleveland*.

Palmi felt that the *Odin* was now sailing more normally, with the wind and waves behind her.

"I noticed that when the wind dropped, the build-up of ice was reduced. It had been at its worst at about the time when the *Notts County* ran aground and the *Ross Cleveland* went down, something more than twelve hours earlier.

Deckhand Torfi Geirmundsson chopping ice aboard the Odin.

❏ Valdimar Jonsson

The Odin, *just after the rescued men from the* Notts County *had been brought aboard. The Zodiac boat used for the rescue lies alongside.*

❏ Valdimar Jonsson

When we got to Isafjord, we saw that so much snow had fallen in the town that the roads were all but impassable. But work had started on clearing the snow. Telephone and electric wires had been damaged. On the dock, an ambulance, a police car and several other vehicles were waiting to take the rescued men to the hospital. A number of people had gathered there to see them."

Skipper Sigurdur spoke to Skipper Burres. At that moment he had no idea that they would ever meet again:

"When I met the captain of the *Notts County*, I immediately sensed he was under enormous stress. He seemed to be finding his feet again after their terrible ordeal. He'd lost one of his crew, as well as his ship. I was sorry to see him looking so poorly— frostbitten and unwell. 'I'll never go to sea again,' he said.

When we got to Isafjord, and most of the crew of the *Notts County* were on the dock, they gathered in a group below the bridge wings, and cheered for us, the crew of the *Odin*. They were thanking us for saving their lives. Exhausted as they were, they had the energy to do that."

Captain Burres had declared on arrival in Isafjord that he would never go to sea again. He was close to collapse.

One of the crew of the *Notts County* was still aboard the *Odin*. First mate Sigurjon was taking care of him:

"Ulfur Gunnarsson, the medical director at the regional hospital, came aboard to examine the men. One of the men said his leg was hurting: 'I think it's broken,' he said.

'Can we get a stretcher aboard to take him off?' asked Ulfur.

'No, that's not really possible. We've only got bulky stretchers, and you can't manoeuvre them down the gangways aboard,' I said. Then I asked:

'Is he too badly injured to be carried off the ship onto the dock? There's an ambulance there, isn't there?'

'Oh, yes,' the doctor replied. 'That should be all right. If someone feels up to carrying him.'

I decided to take care of it. I swung the Englishman up on my back, then carried him up the companionways, along the boat deck, down the gangway and onto the dock. Then he got into the ambulance, I said goodbye, and he was taken up to the hospital."

The people of Hull were in shock. The news of the loss of the *Ross Cleveland* the previous evening had spread like wildfire through the port. A third trawler, lost in the northern seas—and on this occasion in Isafjord Bay, where the crew had sought shelter, believing themselves safe there. The families of the crew were paralyzed with shock. Rita Eddom, Harry's wife, who heard the news at their home in Cottingham, faced the loss of her husband, like many another seaman's wife. At 11:30 a.m. she had been informed that her husband had gone down with his ship.

Lil Bilocca and the other women activists were in London with their petition signed by over 10,000 people, demanding action from the government. Christine Smallbone, the sister of Captain Philip Gay on the *Ross Cleveland*, had intended to go to London with Lil Bilocca, but when she received the news from Iceland of the fate of the trawler and of her brother, she collapsed in shock.

A total of fifty-nine men had been lost, all on trawlers from Hull, except for one from Grimsby. Twelve of the nineteen men on the *Ross Cleveland* were married, and most of them had children. Flags flew at half-mast on the Humber, and around the United Kingdom.

Joseph Mallalieu, minister for shipping at the Board of Trade, said: "Yet again, I have received tragic news. We cannot hold out any hope for the ship or her crew. I have ordered an immediate enquiry into this accident at sea."

* * *

At Isafjord, the trawler *Kingston Garnet* had docked. Her captain, John Lee, had lost his brother on the *Kingston Peridot* when she went down at the end of January. He and his crew had also been in mortal danger that night out on Isafjord Bay. Lee, who was around forty and had been fishing off Iceland for nineteen years, had seen his vessel lay over on her starboard side. He had been sure that he and his crew would share the fate of the men on the *Ross Cleveland*. He turned the ship bow to wind. He feared that she could not right herself but, mercifully, she did.

The trawler *Kingston Andalusite* had also docked at Isafjord. When the crew learned of the rescue of the crew of the *Notts County*, they found it hard to believe that it had been possible to take the men off the ship in the conditions that night.

Among the missing was a lad whose nine brothers and sisters now mourned. Another member of the crew had planned to stay at home in Hull until March, when he was to be married—the vessel owners had asked him to take this extra tour.

Gudmundur Gudmundsson of the Life-Saving Association in Isafjord, together with Captain Halfdan Einarsson of Bolungarvik, had been organizing a search by boats around Isafjord Bay, to find out whether anyone had survived from the *Ross Cleveland* or the *Heidrun II*. Among the vessels used in the search was the *Solrun* from Bolungarvik; one of the places she searched was a small fjord named Seydisfjord, east of Isafjord—not to be confused with the larger fjord of the same name on Iceland's east coast. When the *Solrun* sailed into the fjord, visibility was poor and weather conditions difficult.

Engineer Jon Ragnarsson from the village of Sudavik had been called out to take part in the search:

"I'd heard the communications on the boat frequency when the *Heidrun* sailed out of Bolungarvik on the Sunday. Captain

Under police escort, "Big Lil" Bilocca leads a phalanx of seamen's wives down to the St. Andrew's Docks in Hull on Monday February 5, 1968, when news had been received of the loss of the Ross Cleveland.

❑ Dark Winter—The Hull Daily Mail

Meeting of trawlermen's wives in Bevin House, Hull. Left to right: Mary Deness, Christine Smallbone (sister of Philip Gay, skipper of the Ross Cleveland), *Dorothy Leadbetter, and Teresa Gay (Philip Gay's widow).*

❑ Dark Winter—The Hull Daily Mail

Leifur Jonsson had intended to go, but didn't manage to get aboard. The skipper, Jon Eggert Sigurgeirsson, was caught in the bad weather.

When Leifur was setting off from home, a snowdrift collapsed into his house, and he had to dig his way out. This delayed him, and it meant he missed leaving with the *Heidrun*. That evening I heard Rögnvaldur aboard the *Heidrun*. He said that when they tried to sail into the wind at a light buoy, they lost sight of it because the trawlers around them were all using their arc lights. It was confusing in the poor visibility. I'd also heard the coastguard vessel trying to raise the *Heidrun II*. There was no mention of an emergency aboard, but from the tone of Rögnvaldur's voice I could tell he was uneasy."

Agust Gardarsson of Sudavik was one of those who was assigned to search the shoreline with Jon Ragnarsson in Alftafjord and Seydisfjord on the Monday:

"We went out on the boat *Dröfn* from Sudavik, across the fjord to Kambsneseyri. We went ashore in a dinghy. The weather was so wild that the waves tossed us five or six metres up the beach. We were simply washed ashore. It took all our efforts to prevent our being washed out again by the next wave—we jumped overboard and beached the boat. There was a powerful undertow."

Jon did not like what he saw:

"Ragnar Thorbergsson was with Agust and me. When we got ashore we walked out around the headland. Halfway between the Kambnes headland and the farm of Eyrar, we found a lifebelt and some other stuff. It was clearly from the *Ross Cleveland*.

The weather was so appalling that we had no option but to turn back. They fetched us from the *Dröfn*. The sea in Alftafjord was choppy, too, which is unusual. That day the body of one of the men off the British trawler had been found just outside Sudavik. Another party had been searching under Sjötunahlid in Alftafjord and found another body at the east of the fjord."

In Isafjord harbour, the coastguards were hard at work, chopping ice off the superstructure to make the *Odin* seaworthy once more. Among the men out on deck was Sigurjon:

"On the Monday afternoon we were finishing chopping the ice off the ship as she lay by the dock. On the starboard side was a rowing boat. We had cleared it, all but the ice under it to the side. You couldn't reach that part. There were two stays on the boat, and we'd broken up the ice on both sides of them. Then three or four of us sat under the keel of the boat and pushed at the ice lump with our feet, so it went overboard. When it fell, the ship rolled by at least one or one-and-a-half degrees.

I thought; 'I wonder how much ice we were carrying at the worst, out in the bay last night?

An hour and a half after the crew of the *Notts County* went ashore, we were still hacking the ice off the ship and shoving it overboard. Then I saw a man come sauntering down the dock. When I saw who it was it gave me a strange feeling. 'Am I seeing things?' I asked myself, and stared at the man, to be sure I wasn't mistaken.

'Is it possible?'

It was. It was the man from the *Notts County* I had carried out of the mess and all the way down onto the quay just a little while earlier! There he was, wearing boots, bib overalls and a light-grey speckled woollen sweater.

Here he was, looking fit as a fiddle!

I didn't really want to talk to him anymore. We hadn't had any sleep, and we were worn out—far too tired to give full-grown men piggy-backs up and down ladders for no good reason. When I saw him come walking back on his own two feet, it was too much for me. I'd been working continuously clearing ice, and it was getting on for two days since I'd had a wink of sleep. I'd had enough."

It looked as if most of the *Odin's* crew would now be able to rest for a while—all but Valdimar Jonsson:

"As I watched the crew of the *Notts County* go ashore, I had no idea which of them was the radio operator I'd been talking to all that night and morning. He just went ashore at Isafjord with the rest. That evening most of the crew were allowed to get some sleep, after most of the ice had been cleared off the ship. But I had to set up the aerials ready for the next trip. I was lucky enough to get Grimur Jonsson from Isafjord, who had been a radio operator with the coastguard, to help me out. We fetched some buoy wire, and decided to fit that instead of copper wire.

I'd hardly slept for 48 hours."

It was Monday evening. In Seydisfjord, search parties on the *Solrun* had been looking for traces of the capsized trawler and the *Heidrun II*, but had found nothing in the inner reaches of the fjord.

The life raft where the bodies of Barry Rogers and Wally Hewitt lay was on the eastern shore of the fjord; the nearest farm, Kleifar, was more than four kilometres away, and in any case Harry Eddom had no idea it was there. The farmhouse had no exterior lighting—just the dim glow of oil-lamps in the south-facing windows. But Harry had, earlier in the day, spotted lights on the farm of Eyri, on the opposite shore of the fjord. He knew he had no hope of reaching it on his own.

The route from Lækir, where the life raft was washed ashore, to Kleifahvammur, about a kilometre along the shore of the fjord, is a difficult one, over rough territory, unless you can follow the paths. It is possible to walk along the shore-line for much of the way, but after passing Kleifahvammur a stretch of near-impassable rocks needs to be crossed to reach the head of the fjord.

Headlines in daily Visir *February 5, 1968: "Two British Trawlers Lost" and "Blizzard in north and northwest."*

When Harry had beached the life raft some time on Monday afternoon, he first decided to head north along the shore, then changed his mind and walked southwards, away from the mouth of the fjord.

Harry had to take action, if he was not to die where he stood. It was do or die. He had lost all hope of survival during his long hours in the life raft. Now he was on dry land, admittedly, but the chance of survival seemed slim, in what appeared to be an uninhabited fjord.

And Harry had no idea what to expect, as he began to clamber over ice-sheathed boulders and slippery scree.

Although nearly a day and a night had passed since the *Ross Cleveland* went down, and Harry was himself rimed with frost, soaked to the skin, with his boots half-full of sea water—he was still alive, at least.

Night had fallen in Seydisfjord. Harry had climbed up a rocky cliff near the head of the fjord. At one point he found himself in difficulties; he could no longer follow the shore, and had to climb up a cliff that reached out into the sea. He made his painful way onwards, alone, swept by the icy gale—fighting a lonely battle with death:

"I had to drag myself along—my feet felt as if they were coming off—until I could go no further."

Back home in the United Kingdom, the evening papers were on the newsstands. The *Grimsby Telegraph* quoted a spokesman for the owners of the *Ross Cleveland* as saying that no distress call had been heard from the ship before she sank. "They would have had no time to launch life rafts," he said. The newspaper went on to report that "conditions were so severe that the Icelandic rescue services, claimed to be the best in the Northern hemisphere, were brought to a halt."

William Howbrigg, cook on the *Ross Cleveland*, who had been put ashore at Isafjord in January because he was ill, was back in Hull by now. He had had a lucky escape.

George Burres, the skipper of the *Notts County*, and first mate Barry Stokes had been admitted to hospital in Isafjord with frostbite. The first mate also had a sprained ankle, and the captain was suffering from shock. They were to stay there for some time.

Harry Eddom could hardly move his legs. Shaking, deprived of sleep, running out of hope, he was at the end of his tether. He had had nothing to eat or drink for twenty-four hours. He was approaching a white-painted summer cabin by a brook at the head of Seydisfjord:

The trawler disasters in Isafjord Bay reported in the British press.

"I came to a sort of deserted farmhouse and tried to break in, but it was all shuttered up. I hadn't the strength to kick the door open—my legs were frozen. I got into the lee-side cover of the house and just stood there. I couldn't go any further because it was dark.

I knew that if I sat down and fell asleep I would just freeze. I stood up all night. I lost count of time as I stood there. But I knew I had to stay awake. Every time I felt myself dozing off I clapped my hands to restore the circulation.

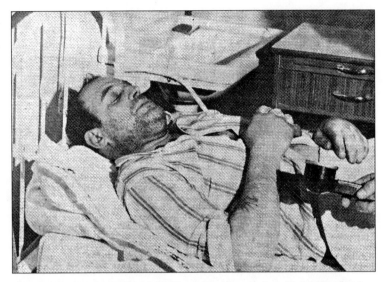

George Burres, captain of the Notts County, *in hospital in Isafjord. He had played an active part in chopping the ice off the trawler in the freak storm, and refused to let his crew lose hope as they waited for rescue.*

❏ Bj. Pálsson

I kept telling myself: 'You've got to keep awake, you've got to keep awake.'

I just kept hoping and hoping that someone would come."

It was Tuesday morning.

The night had passed, and still no one knew that one man from the *Ross Cleveland* was desperately hanging on to life under the eaves of a summer cabin in Seydisfjord. Harry, like the rest of the crew, was believed to have gone down with the ship. The Icelandic media reported that the *Ross Cleveland* had been lost with all hands, that one man had died and eighteen had been rescued from the *Notts County*, and that the crew of the *Heidrun II* were missing.

In Hull, and all around the United Kingdom, the tragic news caused uproar.

In Isafjord, the coastguards on the *Odin* were preparing to return to the *Notts County* to retrieve the body of 23-year-old Robert Bowie. Most of the ice had been cleared off the superstructure of the coastguard vessel. Torfi Geirmundsson went ashore briefly:

"I dashed up to the Scouts' hostel with some clothes the rescued men had left aboard the coastguard vessel when they'd taken them off wet the day before. I met two of the men from the *Notts County*, who I'd talked to in the mess after the rescue.

But when I went to say hello to them, I realized they didn't recognize me. I understood even more clearly than before that they'd been in deep shock when they boarded the ship. I said hello, and they nodded to me, looking bemused, as if they were wondering who I was."

The *Odin* headed north for Snæfjallaströnd. The diesel engine of the *Odin's* covered boat was started, and Sigurjon and Palmi returned to the grounded ship. The layer of ice on the outside of the bridge was forty centimetres thick. Sigurjon entered the bridge:

"When we got into the bridge of the *Notts County* we saw that two of the windows were slightly open. Clearly, snow must have been getting in while the men were waiting to be rescued.

Between the bulwark and the superstructure of the trawler, snow had fallen and frozen, so the gap was completely full. We'd been told that the dead man was lying just fore of the derrick on the port side, so we started to dig him out by chopping the ice away. But we had to be careful.

Daily Morgunblaðið
February 6, 1968:
"British parliament shocked at news of disasters off Iceland."

Daily Morgunblaðið:
"Heidrun Missing."

First we dug our way down to the life raft, then pulled the ice away. There was practically no air left in the raft, it was just like a bit of sailcloth. When we lifted it up, the body was left lying on the deck. I thought it was strange that the man had been left out there."

Torfi Geirmundsson could see that the fate of the young Englishman angered Sigurjon. When the body had been lifted up

Coastguard ship Odin *and the grounded trawler* Notts County.

❏ Bragi Guðmundsson

A boat from the Odin *lies alongside the ice-covered* Notts County, *on the coastguards' second visit to the vessel, to fetch the body of Robert Bowie.*

❏ Bragi Guðmundsson

The Zodiac boat returns to the Odin *from the* Notts County *(far left) on the second trip to the grounded trawler.*

❏ Valdimar Jonsson

onto the *Odin's* helicopter landing pad, the sailcloth that had covered him fluttered in the wind. As Torfi looked into the face of the young man, and his long, frozen hair, the thought of this man dying of cold sent a shiver down his spine.

To the east of Skutulsfjord and the village of Isafjord lies Alftafjord. The next fjord is Seydisfjord, which was at that time accessible only by sea. At the head of Seydisfjord on the western side was the farm of Kleifar, home of sixty-year-old Gudmundur Asgeirsson and his wife Karitas Gudbjörg Gudlaugsdottir. Of their twelve children, six were still living at home when the freak storm struck Isafjord Bay—Haraldur was fifteen, Gudmann fourteen, Gudrun twelve, Bardur seven, Olafur five, and Solrun four years old. The elder siblings had all moved away. The farm's livestock comprised 180 sheep, four cows and four horses. Haraldur and Gudmann had been at school until the age of fourteen, when they returned home to help on the farm. They generally began the day by fetching water from the brook for the cows and horses, while the sheep were let out to graze. But at this time of year, when everything was covered in snow, it could be difficult to get to the water.

Coastguards aboard the Notts County *the day after the rescue, to fetch the body of Robert Bowie.*

In Seydisfjord the snow was much thicker on the western side of the fjord, and so the boys generally drove the sheep around the head of the fjord—past the summer cabin where Harry Eddom had taken shelter the previous evening—to the eastern side, where the grazing was better. This was Kleifarhvammur, where Harry had clambered up the rocks on the Monday. About a kilometre beyond the headland, Harry's life raft had been washed ashore.

Fourteen-year-old Gudmann could hardly believe the weather they had seen over the past two days:

"It was my job to take the sheep out to pasture, but that hadn't been possible since Saturday. My brother Haraldur and I were also supposed to milk the cows, and water them and the horses. All day Sunday there had been a blizzard. Dad had fed the sheep and cows, while my brother and I fed the horses. The cowshed was only a short distance from the farmhouse, but we couldn't see it from the house for the snow. You couldn't see your hand in front of your face. We had to find our way by memory when we went out to the cowshed.

Kleifar, Seydisfjord.

By Monday morning we were running short of water for the animals. We had to make our way out and dig through a load of snow to get water from the brook. The gully above the farm was completely full of snow.

The weather didn't really start to die down until Monday afternoon. We'd heard on the radio what had been happening out in the bay. But on the Sunday the phone lines in the fjord had come down, due to icing. So we had no phone contact with the outside world."

The morning was wearing on. At Kleifar in Seydisfjord, Gudmundur was feeding the cows and sheep. Gudmann and Haraldur had had some coffee in the kitchen before joining their father. They saw that the water level in the cows' troughs was low.

As the sun rose, Gudmann thought that it would be possible to drive the sheep around the fjord to Kleifahvammur to pasture.

The blizzard had abated.

"After milking we went indoors and had breakfast: porridge and blood pudding. It was past ten when we went back out. We hadn't let any of the animals out on Sunday or Monday, and had to feed them indoors both morning and evening. By the time we went to sleep on Monday evening, the weather was fine.

I went down the slope on the farm, to fetch the sheep. I had two dogs with me, old Nikulas and his son Mori. I was going to take the sheep around the head of the fjord to the other side. When I got to the head of the fjord, the sheep ran on ahead of me around Fjardarhorn. I thought the weather was fine, compared with what we'd just had—the temperature was above freezing and there was a light breeze blowing. I was thinking about my brother Olafur—it was his eighth birthday. That meant Mum would make pancakes later on.

I'd walked along the shore around the head of the fjord, and past the summer cabin, which stood on a gravel ridge just above the high-water mark. Suddenly I saw footprints. 'Could it be one of the shipwrecked men?' I immediately thought. 'Did someone survive?'

The footprints were quite deep. The man had been wading calf-deep through the snow. It was clearly a grown man. But the footprints seemed closely spaced—he hadn't been taking big steps.

The dogs started barking, and they both came running towards me. At that moment I turned around and heard someone calling out to me. I realized at once it was a foreign language that I didn't understand.

I went towards the man who was standing by the wall of the summer cabin. It didn't take me long to realize what had happened. He had to be a survivor from the sunken British trawler."

Just about thirty-six hours had passed since the *Ross Cleveland* vanished into the depths of Isafjord Bay. Something incomprehensible had happened. Harry Eddom, though more dead than alive, had survived.

Kleifar. Gudmann Gudmundsson (centre) with his parents, Gudmundur and Gudbjörg, and younger siblings.

"When daylight came I was that frozen, I couldn't move my legs or anything. And in the morning I saw a shepherd boy—he was only a young lad—and shouted to him. He ran over to me."

Gudmann observed Harry, a dark, powerfully built man below average height, wearing a duck suit and boots, like any trawlerman. Harry realized at once that the boy's arrival had saved his life, and Gudmann, too, was aware of this.

Both were overcome with joy:

"The man was on his last legs. He was so pleased to see me. His face lit up. I didn't know how long he'd been there, but his footprints were clear—the snow hadn't drifted since he got there. When we went out to do the milking the previous evening, about nine, the weather had changed for the better. So he couldn't have got to the house before that.

He tried to talk to me, but I couldn't understand a word. He was exhausted, and he was stiff and unsteady on his feet. I had to hold him up. He didn't have any gloves, but he was wearing waders, and a bluish anorak with a hood—which didn't look waterproof to me, although I wasn't sure."

Gudmann and Harry stood by the south wall of the house. The footprints in the snow indicated that Harry had stood at a point that was sheltered from the wind—and also out of sight of the farmhouse at Kleifar. So Harry didn't know there was a farm close by, with no lights during the night. He simply awaited his fate, by a summer cabin that was rarely visited in winter. When the sun came up, Harry could have looked around the corner of the house and seen the farmhouse only one-and-a-half kilometres away. The lights he had seen when the life raft washed ashore were at Eyri, farther out along the fjord. He could never have reached there without help, as he was well aware.

"I put my arm around him and held under his right arm. He placed his left arm over my shoulders, and we made our way slowly home to Kleifar. We went down to the shore, then on to the farm. It was some distance. He tried to talk to me.

'I don't understand,' I said in Icelandic.

He soon gave up, when he realized I didn't understand. And he was quite exhausted, too."

Harry felt, more clearly than before, how close to death he had come. If no one had come along he would have died within a short time. His condition was poor:

"I was so dead beat and my feet were hurting so much I couldn't walk. The lad had to half-carry me to his parents' farmhouse."

Soon Harry spotted the house they were headed for. Although it was not far away, Harry could never have made it on his own.

The farmhouse at Kleifar stands on a slope, and the path from the shore to the house is all uphill, along a river gorge and across the homefield. Gudmann had his hands full helping Harry up the slope through the snow drifts.

"When we got to the homefield, my father noticed I was helping a man towards the farm. He hurried down to us to assist us. Then we helped him up to the house.

When we got indoors we took the shipwrecked man into the kitchen and helped him out of his wet clothes. He took off his anorak, then pulled off his high boots. It was difficult. The boots were stuck fast, and when my father and I finally freed them, sea water poured out. The man was soaked.

I could hardly believe he didn't have any gloves on. Under his anorak he was wearing a thick woolly sweater, and a warm shirt. Under the trousers he was wearing long woollen underwear. He had thin woollen socks on his feet. He didn't seem warmly enough dressed to have survived being shipwrecked, and then standing for hours in the cold without moving."

Harry Eddom had never in his life been so glad to see anyone as the people on the farm of Kleifar. When Gudmann had brought him into the warmth of his parents' home, Harry realized that he was indeed safe at last, with farmer Gudmundur and Gudbjörg, his kind and motherly wife.

Thirty-six hours after the trawler sank into the icy seas, Harry was finally beginning to think he would be all right. During those long hours, he had come to believe that he would certainly die:

"When we got to the house his mother and father stripped off my frozen clothing and gave me three cups of coffee. Never has coffee tasted so good."

Harry was starting to relax, after having forced himself to stay awake all night and into the morning. Gudmann saw that Harry's eyelids were beginning to droop:

"I saw when he got into the warmth indoors that he was very weak, and he was still very cold. We dressed him in thick long cotton underpants, jeans, a vest, a shirt and a sweater. We also gave him food and drink, and he ate and drank well. Then he lay down on the couch in the kitchen, which was the warmest part of the house. As soon as he lay back, he fell fast asleep."

The telephone line to Kleifar was still down after the storm, so the extraordinary news of Harry Eddom's survival could not yet be passed on. All the family at Kleifar could do was wait. They knew that search parties were out. But the most important thing was that the Englishman was alive, and on his way to recovery.

The search party included, as before, Jon Ragnarsson and Agust Gardarsson from Sudavik, who had gone into Seydisfjord with the boat *Svanur*. The *Solrun* had been there on the Monday, but without spotting the life raft—and at that time visibility had still been poor. The skipper of the *Svanur* was Thorir Hinriksson.

The engineer was Jon Ragnarsson:

"We'd put some men ashore at Folafot, the headland between Seydisfjord and Hestfjord, then gone on into Seydisfjord. The weather was fine by then. Suddenly we noticed a life raft—inflated, on dry land. It looked as if it had washed ashore nearly a kilometre outside Hruteyri, on the east of the fjord.

We put out a dinghy, and some of the lads went ashore. As they rowed towards the life raft, they saw footprints in the snow, leading away from the raft towards the screes farther up the fjord. The man seemed to have clambered up there, then turned back. When the lads followed the tracks, they saw that the man appeared to have lain down in a hollow up by a rock.

To judge from the traces in the snow, he seemed to have lain on his back with his arms stretched out, making a cross-shaped mark in the snow.

We knew that if he'd headed towards the sea he wouldn't have had a chance. There was no habitation there, nor any shelter of any kind. He'd walked out along the fjord for a bit, but then he seemed to have realized he was making a mistake, and turned back the other way, into the fjord.

In the life raft we found two bodies, which were mostly submerged.

One of the men was wearing a blue woollen sweater and trousers. The other was even more poorly dressed, wearing only underwear. The one who was wearing more seemed to be rather older. The other was heavily tattooed. Both bodies were stiff, in a sitting position. But we managed to straighten the bodies out to lay them on the starboard side of the deck, and covered them with blankets. It was a grisly task, but it's something you have to face in rescue work.

We thought that the man who had left the footprints in the snow might have tried to get to Kleifar."

Agust Gardarsson considered whether the man could have made his way up the fjord, and how:

"The route to Kleifar from the place where the life raft was beached is very rugged and hard going, even in summer. So I thought the man could hardly have gone that way in the dark. If you're not familiar with the territory, you just couldn't get across there in the pitch dark, especially if you were exhausted to start with."

They took the *Svanur* into the fjord. Jon Ragnarsson prepared to go ashore with the other men in a small boat:

"We decided to go to Kleifar. When we put the dinghy out and rowed ashore, we were in a state of suspense. Had the trawlerman really escaped from the horrors of the past few days? Some bodies had been found in Isafjord Bay, but now there was a chance of finding someone alive. We were astonished.

When we got to the farmhouse, we met Gudmann and the family. They told us the British trawlerman was indoors. I was eager to see him. They said he had lain down in the kitchen. He was dazed and seemed tired, but otherwise appeared to be in good condition. He didn't seem to be in any great discomfort, astonishing as that seemed. We thought he was likely to have frostbite. So we decided to get him over to Isafjord to a doctor at once."

Harry had only slept for just over two hours in the kitchen at Kleifar when the search party arrived. It seemed astonishing that he was able to wake up to go out to the *Svanur*. Agust was one of the men at Kleifar:

"When I looked at him, he seemed to be very warmly dressed. The people at the farm had clearly taken great care to dress him well. I was especially interested to see that they had even put woollen mittens on his hands. I looked at the clothes he'd been wearing when found—waders, and over-the-knee woollen socks."

Gudmann felt that Harry, whom he had half-carried home only a short time earlier, had made a remarkable recovery after his brief rest. Gudmann watched as coffee and the birthday pancakes were served to Harry and the men from the *Svanur*. Captain Thorir Hinriksson knew a little English, and he talked to the rescued man.

Gudmann had seen the *Solrun* come into Seydisfjord on the Monday, at around dusk. The storm was dying down by that time, and the wind had dropped to about force 6 or 7. That was about the time the life raft was washing ashore with Harry aboard, but no one saw it then.

Now it was time to take Harry to Isafjord. The rescue team knew that Harry's return from the dead would arouse huge media interest. People would find it almost impossible to believe that anyone could survive an ordeal such as Harry's—for 36 hours after he was believed dead. Agust and the team made preparations to transport Harry:

"We'd come ashore from the *Svanur* in a dinghy, and I saw that he seemed a bit taken aback when we took him on board the boat. The dinghy was so small that we had to put the stretcher athwart, with the ends projecting over the gunwale on both sides. One man sat aft with him, and the others were forward, rowing. I'd noticed at Kleifar that he had damage to his hands and feet from the cold."

When they reached the *Svanur*, engineer Jon observed Harry, where he had been settled down in the captain's cabin:

"He was warmly wrapped up. And he was well enough to talk to skipper Thorir:

He told Thorir what had happened. He knew we had collected his shipmates' bodies, and that they were on board with us. He believed they'd pulled him into the life raft. He said they'd died on the Sunday night—they couldn't keep warm enough.

It had been light when the life raft washed ashore. He described his walk to the summer cabin, and said he had intended to break into the cabin, but hadn't had the strength.

He was in extraordinarily good condition physically. He was very calm, and he didn't seem to be suffering any after-effects, in spite of the appalling physical and emotional ordeal he had been through. He made a good impression.

When we sailed into Skutulsfjord and to Isafjord harbour, there were many British trawlers there. It was a sad sight. All the ships were thickly sheathed in ice."

The *Svanur* approached the dock. The amazing news had spread that one of the crew of the *Ross Cleveland* had been found, alive. The *Svanur* had sent notification that they were bringing the man in to Isafjord, so that he could be picked up and taken to hospital.

When the boat docked, many men from the crews of the other British trawlers formed a guard of honour. Agust Gardarsson noticed, as they brought the rescued man ashore, that he closely observed his fellow-countrymen and the trawlers.

In Isafjord, Alan Bennett, a journalist with the *Daily Express*, had just arrived. He was interviewing the men who had been rescued off the *Notts County*, who were in the Scouts' hostel. Suddenly an Icelandic seaman burst in, and called out:

"There's a man from the *Ross Cleveland*—and he's alive!"

Bennett could not believe his ears. Without losing a moment, he rushed out into the snowy streets and down to the harbour. The *Svanur* was coming in. An ambulance was brought up to the boat. And Alan saw powerfully built seamen lift a man on a stretcher. He was bare-headed, wearing an anorak he had been lent at Kleifar.

A deckhand from one of the other Hull trawlers was on the dock, watching. His eyes seemed to be bursting out of his head as he recognized the man on the stretcher:

"My God, that's Harry Eddom! It's like looking at a ghost!" exclaimed the man.

The news spread like wildfire around Isafjord that one of the crew of the Ross Cleveland *had been found, alive. A crowd gathered on the dock when he was brought ashore.*

❏ Jón Aðalbjörn Bjarnason (þjóðviljinn)

Thorir Hinriksson, the skipper of the *Svanur*, remarked that Harry Eddom had "showed more courage than I would ever have believed possible." Harry was taken to the regional hospital in Isafjord, where he was placed in the care of Dr. Ulfur Gunnarsson, who together with the other hospital staff had looked after the captain and first mate of the *Notts County* the previous day. But before any treatment commenced for Harry's injuries, it was time to ring his family with the incredible news—he was alive!

All his relatives in Hull believed he was lost at sea.

The international telephone operator in Reykjavik was given Harry's home number in Cottingham, where Rita Eddom was at home with their little daughter. Harry was sitting in a wheelchair

Harry Eddom arrives at Isafjord.

Aboard the Svanur. *Harry Eddom being carried off the boat at Isafjord. In the foreground, the life raft in which Harry was tossed around on the sea, with two of his shipmates from the* Ross Cleveland.

in a corridor of the hospital. He was sluggish with exhaustion, and in pain from his frostbitten hands and feet. He sat with the receiver in his hand, waiting to be put through.

*British trawlers in
harbour at Isafjord
after the storm.*
❏ Bragi Guðmundsson

Strangely, there was no answer. Harry was told that no one
had answered at his home. Wasn't Rita in? He couldn't wait—he
simply had to tell his family himself that he was alive, before it
was on the news back home.

Now Harry asked to be connected to his parents' home. This
time, the attempt was successful.

"Phone call from Iceland," he heard on the line.

Michael Eddom, Harry's brother, was two years his junior.
He was training to be an engineer. He was at their parents' home.
Initially, Michael assumed that the call from Iceland was to in-
form them that his brother's body had been found.

"Hello, Michael, it's me," said Harry hoarsely.

Michael, who had believed for the past twenty-four hours that
his brother was dead, did not recognize the voice on the phone,
and assumed this was a grim hoax.

Harry realized what was happening:

"'If this is a joke, it's not funny,' Michael angrily retorted.

'No, Michael, it's me. Your brother, Harry!' I said.

There was silence on the line. They he asked:

'Where on earth are you ringing from?'

131

'Michael. I'm in hospital in Isafjord. I'm all right. I'm fine,' I said.

I realised that Michael felt as if he were talking to someone from another planet. He was speechless. I told him about the rescue, and said I hadn't been able to get through to Rita.

'Go over to her now, will you, and tell her about me. I'll talk to her later,' I said."

The brothers said their goodbyes. Michael gave his elderly parents the incredible good news. Minnie, Harry's mother, came on the line:

Minnie, who could hardly speak, asked tearfully: "Are you all right, son?"

Harry replied: "Yes, I'm all right, Mom. How are you?"

Michael decided to hurry over to give Rita the news.

When Michael stood at Rita's door, it transpired that she had been home when the call was made. But she could not believe what she heard.

"I won't believe it till I hear Harry myself," she said, trembling with joy and fear and astonishment. What was happening? An hour later she still had not managed to reach Harry on the phone. Journalists were gathering at her home. Rita was impatient. She could not wait any longer to find out what had happened. When she finally made contact with Harry, he said:

"The ship turned over, and my mates went."

When Rita heard her husband's voice, she burst into tears. She had not dared believe he was alive, until she heard his voice herself.

The day before, when she was informed that the *Ross Cleveland* had gone down, Rita had said there was no God. "But I believe in him now," she said, weeping.

She bombarded her husband with questions:

Harry Eddom in hospital at Isafjord, giving the good news to his brother in Hull. Nurse Ketty Roesen in the background.

❏ Tíminn

"Harry, is it really you? I can't believe it. How are you? Where are you? Are you hurt?"

She said she had no idea why Harry had not been able to get through to her earlier that day. She had not been out of the house. The couple spoke for six minutes, and decided to speak again when he had had some rest.

Dr. Ulfur, who had commented that Harry's survival was almost beyond belief, informed him that it might prove necessary to amputate some toes. But they would wait and see how Harry was tomorrow. Harry was given an injection, and went off to sleep.

Rita Eddom had an emotional reunion to look forward to over the phone. And there were many outsiders who wanted to observe that event—and were already making their plans.

That evening, Lil Bilocca returned from her trip to London, with Mary Deness and Yvonne Blenkinsop.

Big Lil had burst out crying when she heard the news that one of the *Ross Cleveland*'s crew, Harry Eddom, had been found alive. "I'd give ten years of my life if the other men who were lost on the trawler could be found too."

The women's mission had yielded results.

"We've won, lads. We've won!" Big Lil called out on her return to her home town. "I've never been so happy in my life."

Mary Deness commented: "Three women have achieved more in one day than anything that has ever been done in the trawler industry in sixty years!"

Yvonne Blenkinsop said: "Our men are good men. They want to take good care of their wives, but we'll get them to rise up and defend themselves."

The authorities in London had promised a public enquiry into the loss of the ships off Iceland. They had also given an undertaking that seamen's safety would be thoroughly reviewed.

In spite of these declarations, British seamen were so shocked by the events off Iceland that it was proving difficult to man the trawlers of Hull and Grimsby.

When the news spread throughout the United Kingdom that one man had survived the terrible events off Iceland, after having been believed dead for 36 hours, practically every journalist in the country wanted to interview him.

They were literally out of control.

Icelandic journalists had been told that Harry could not be interviewed yet—he must be left to rest without disturbance.

That evening, journalists at the *Sun* had a bright idea. Obviously, Rita Eddom was desperate to see her husband. The editorial board decided to make her an offer—the paper would give her an all-expenses-paid trip to Iceland. She could even take

Harry's parents and her baby daughter along. And she would also be paid a fee. In return, the *Sun* wanted an exclusive interview, and an exclusive photograph of the couple when they were reunited at the hospital in Isafjord.

Rita did not have much money—the Eddoms had a mortgage to pay on their new home. The journalists were persistent, and eventually Rita agreed to their terms. Her first priority was to see Harry.

Iceland's Prime Minister, Bjarni Benediktsson, sent a telegram to Prime Minister Harold Wilson:

> On my behalf and that of the Government of Iceland, I extend to you, the British people, and particularly the families concerned, the deepest condolences on the grievous loss of lives sustained by the British trawler fleet in the recent disasters in northern waters.

Mr. Wilson replied by telegram, thanking the Icelandic Prime Minister for his sympathetic message. He promised to pass on his condolences to the families of those who had perished, and said that it would be especially meaningful to them, coming from a nation so familiar with the perils of the northern seas. He went on to thank the Icelandic nation for their help, and especially the Iceland Coastguard, and the crew of the *Odin* for their selfless bravery. Mr. Wilson's telegram ends with an expression of sympathy to the families of the men lost on the Icelandic boat *Heidrun*.

The Bishop of Iceland, the right Rev. Sigurbjörn Einarsson, also exchanged expressions of sympathy with the Bishop of Hull, the Right Rev. Hall Higgs.

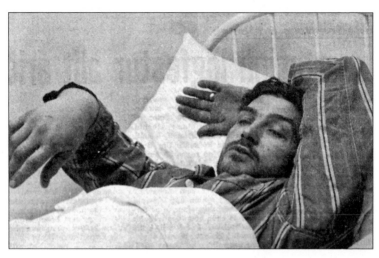

Harry Eddom in hospital in Isafjord.

❑ Högni Torfason

By Wednesday, dozens of British reporters were in Iceland, or on their way. Many were to travel on the same flight as Rita Eddom, by Icelandair from Glasgow to Keflavik. Little Natalee had a cold, so she stayed at home in England with her maternal grandmother.

By now Harry Eddom was well enough to talk to a journalist from the Icelandic afternoon paper *Visir,* from his hospital bed in Isafjord. And a reporter for daily *Morgunbladid* had spoken briefly with Harry the previous day.

When he woke up that morning, he was pleased to hear the doctor say that his toes were in extraordinarily good condition. They had improved greatly since he was admitted to hospital, and no action would be taken for the time being.

"Three women have achieved more in one day than anything that has ever been done in the trawler industry in sixty years!" said Mary Deness, one of the militant seamen's wives who campaigned for improved safety in the British fishing industry.

❏ Dark Winter—The Hull Daily Mail

Rita Eddom with baby Natalee, on the phone at home in Cottingham, at about the time she contacted her husband in hospital in Isafjord.

❏ Dark Winter—The Hull Daily Mail

Harry had no idea of what was going on in England, but he had been informed that his wife was on her way to Isafjord. Harry was taken to the phone in a wheelchair. He was looking forward to seeing Rita. He remarked jokingly:

137

"Hello, pet. I'm fine and the beer here is smashing!"

"That's my Harry!" Rita remarked. "It's like hearing from a ghost."

"Can you walk, Harry?" Rita asked.

"Sort of. But it's more like a hobble. The doctor says my feet will improve in about a fortnight. Rita, I have a bottle of brandy. We'll open it for a celebration when you arrive."

The couple said goodbye. Harry went back into the ward by wheelchair and was helped into bed. When he had lain down, he reached out for a cigarette, lit up, and said: "I can't wait to see Rita."

Dr. Ulfur Gunnarsson told a reporter from the *Evening News* that he had long experience of what the sea and frost could do to a man:

"I had never before known a man to be subjected to such conditions for so long and survive. I think it was his physical condition and, perhaps just as important, his strong will to live which kept him alive. He is a young man and his physical condition is very good. I think he may have to lose a couple of toes—what is that, compared to his life? But even the toes may be saved. When I saw him yesterday, I was sure that two other toes would have to be removed. Today they appear to be improving."

Asked how he came to be in such excellent physical condition, Harry replied that it might be because he had played football. He had had to give it up, admittedly, when he left school and went to sea at the age of 15. Harry added that he also came from a long line of seamen.

Doctor Ulfur could not help becoming aware of the huge interest both Icelandic and foreign press were showing in Harry Eddom. Ulfur suggested to Harry that he could arrange for a private plane to take him secretly back to the United Kingdom, away from the persistent press. Harry simply smiled and shook his head. He was comfortable at the hospital, where we was able to rest, surrounded by helpful staff. Later he was to realize that it might have been a good idea to accept Ulfur's offer.

Sixteen of the crew of the *Notts County* were now preparing to return home. Most had been put up at the Scouts' hostel in Isafjord. Dick Moore was keen to go home. He was determined to see his Norwegian girlfriend:

"The day after we were brought in to Isafjord, we were taken to a clothes shop, and told to choose things to replace the clothes we had lost in the wreck. Most of us picked warm jackets. Then we flew to Reykjavik on the Tuesday, and stayed at a hotel. But Captain Burres and first mate Stokes stayed on for further treatment at the hospital in Isafjord.

When we got to Reykjavik, we received a request for two of us, the radio operator and one other man, to go to a studio for a TV interview which would be sent to London. We wanted to go into town in Reykjavik, maybe even have some fun, but we had no money. And we knew prices were very high in Iceland. But we lacked for nothing—we were always given plenty to eat. The following day, on the Wednesday, we went out to Keflavik Airport for our flight to Glasgow.

When we got off the plane we were met by dozens of photographers and reporters. But we had been told not to talk to any of them. The journalists were kept back behind a fence. They shouted and called out to us, and wanted to interview us, or get some comments on what had happened off Iceland.

The photographers took lots of pictures, but we didn't answer any questions. The police had their hands full keeping the press away from us. We went straight into a coach which took us

Sixteen of the crew of the Notts County *arrive in Reykjavik after their Icelandair flight from Isafjord. Dick Moore is fourth from the right.*

❏ Bragi Guðmundsson

Deckhands Gilbert Cook (centre) and John Davidson from the Notts County *talk to a* Sun *reporter.*

❏ Bragi Guðmundsson

Frank McGuinness, deckhand on the Notts County.

❏ Bragi Guðmundsson

to Grimsby. We didn't even have to go through customs—and of course we had no luggage. On the way to Grimsby we were given a good meal, and most of us felt good. We were happy. After all, we were alive, and on the way home to our loved ones."

Rita Eddom was at Glasgow Airport, after her train journey from Hull. She was to fly to Iceland on the same plane that had brought the crew of the *Notts County* home. About twenty reporters and photographers, the same ones who had clustered around the crew of the *Notts County*, were to fly on the same plane. A BAC 111 was also on its way to Iceland from London, carrying sixteen representatives of the Associated Press news agency. Onward travel to Isafjord was arranged by Icelandair or by private plane.

Extraordinary media attention focused on the young woman from Hull and her husband. Rita was accompanied by her parents-in-law, Harry senior and Minnie, and her twelve-year-old brother, Dennis Penrose. Since seven-month-old Natalee had a cold, Rita had not felt happy about taking her to the chilly north.

The Icelandair Boeing 727 was waiting at the airport to take Rita and her family, as well as journalists and other passengers, to Keflavik. Reporters and "bodyguards" from the *Sun* kept other members of the press away from Rita and the family. The atmosphere was tense.

Rita was in a state of strain brought on by anticipation, fatigue and stress. When she spoke, she was half-laughing, half-crying, yet her joy, and the hope that Harry would be all right, overcame all. But she was surprised by the media attention she received—after all it was her husband who had survived so miraculously—not she.

Isafjord hospital.

❏ Bragi Guðmundsson

Rita had not slept since the Monday—the day she heard of the loss of the *Ross Cleveland*. Initially, she was overcome with grief. Then the incredible good news followed on the Tuesday, followed by a period of uncertainty, waiting, thinking and intrusive media attention.

To Rita, it was like a dream.

She considered whether Harry's ordeal would have changed him. Whether he would still be the same calm, easy-going man she had known.

When the plane landed in Keflavik, chaos broke out. On the way over, the *Sun* reporters had tried to keep reporters from other media away from Rita. But when they entered the small terminal building, they were met by dozens more reporters, both Icelandic and British. Rita was the focus of attention.

Scuffles broke out as the reporters jostled and shoved to reach her. The *Sun* intended sending Rita to Isafjord the following morning, but other reporters had made their own plans. Pilot

Björn Palsson had been engaged to fly them to Isafjord, and they had arranged to have the runway at Isafjord lit up by car headlights. Resourceful reporters from the *Daily Express* tried to trick Rita into their hired plane, pretending to be from the *Sun*.

They almost succeeded.

Turmoil spread throughout the terminal—along corridors, up and down stairs, in all directions. The *Sun* representatives did what they could to shield Rita from their colleagues from other media. "This is a farce," said one of the Icelandic reporters. "You must have forgotten your boxing gloves," replied a colleague. Few members of the Icelandic press had ever seen such a circus.

In the struggle for a news item or a picture, the press were growing desperate, not least because the *Sun* was fiercely guarding its rights over Rita. All the newspaper, TV and radio reporters at the airport had hoped for an interview with her.

But the *Sun*'s men arranged for Rita to take refuge in the ladies' lavatory while chaos reigned outside. Some of the Icelandic reporters felt let down—they thought that Rita could have talked to them, especially since her husband had been rescued by Icelanders.

Rita was happy to speak to anyone who showed an interest in her and Harry. The problem was that it was difficult for her to do so while she was so carefully guarded by the *Sun*. Rita was keen to let the people of Iceland know, via the Icelandic media, of her heartfelt gratitude to those who had saved her husband's life— and not least the young lad on the farm of Kleifar who had found him that Tuesday morning.

The *Sun* representative put Rita in a taxi, and took her to Hotel Saga in downtown Reykjavik. The taxi was followed, but only the *Sun* could interview Rita. The following morning she went to the domestic airport in Reykjavik for her flight to

Harry Eddom's parents, Harry senior and Minnie, arriving in Iceland.
❏ Bragi Guðmundsson

Isafjord, but not before she had spoken to Icelandic reporters, and warmly thanked the Icelanders for saving her husband.

The Icelandair plane took off at about 1 p.m. on the Thursday. The moment had come—Rita was to be reunited with Harry. The reporters were now even more determined than before. At six o'clock that morning they had started gathering at the hospital. Doctor Ulfur Gunnarsson said that either all the press would have to be admitted, or none at all.

And no one would be allowed in if there were any scuffles.

When the plane landed at about 2 p.m. Rita, her brother and Harry's parents were taken out to a car, and driven a complicated route around the town, in order to try to confuse anyone who was following. When the car arrived at the hospital, about fifty members of the media were believed to be waiting there.

Harry Eddom was fairly calm, as he waited in the hospital, but he was a little worried about the swelling of his fingers—he

144

Rita Eddom and her young brother Dennis Penrose on their flight to Iceland.
❏ Morgunblaðið

had been afraid he would not be able to put his wedding ring on before his wife arrived. But he had managed it in the end.

The *Sun* representatives were furious when they learned that all the press were to be admitted—they tried to enter the hospital while keeping the rest out, but without success. There was a scuffle in the hospital entrance. The *Sun* claimed to have exclusive rights to photograph the couple's meeting, and interview them. Doctor Ulfur and other staff had to use force to keep the press outside.

In the confusion, one of the *Sun* reporters managed to enter the hospital. Another reporter from the *Sun*, and a photographer who had been assigned to photograph Rita and Harry's reunion, seized the opportunity and entered by the rear door. They were spotted by a nurse, who tried to stop them, but had to let them go after a struggle that left her bruised. The photographer found his way in to Rita.

Media madness at Keflavik Airport as Rita Eddom departs by car.
❑ Bragi Guðmundsson

The Sun's *reporter leads Rita Eddom to the car which is waiting to take her to Reykjavik. The* Sun *ensured no other reporters could approach Mrs. Eddom.*
❑ Bragi Guðmundsson

But Rita's mind was not on the planned interview. When she entered the ward where Harry lay in bed, she finally looked into his eyes.

"Oh, Rita!" said Harry as he lay in bed. The reporter and photographer from the *Sun* were with them in the ward. The

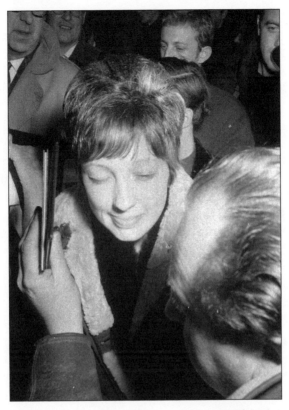

Keflavik Airport. The Sun *reporter helps Rita into the car.*

❑ Bragi Guðmundsson

moment was so emotional that Rita, who had mourned her husband for two days, who had not slept for days, could not speak a word. She burst into tears, and could not even walk over to Harry's bed. He saw how much strain the past few days had been for her.

Rita was helped over to a chair at the other end of the room, so she could recover. She was brought a glass of water, which she sipped as tears poured down her cheeks. She looked at her husband and said:

"I couldn't bear to think you'd drowned. Honestly, deep inside me, I'd lost all hope of ever seeing you again."

"It's all right, love. It's all over now," Harry quietly comforted her.

Rita stood up, wiped away her tears, held out her arms and walked over to Harry, who gave her a big smile. Her long-suffering yet calm husband reached out for her, and Rita bent down, sat by him on the bed, and the young couple kissed warmly.

The clicking of the camera was heard, and flash lights lit the room.

Rita and Harry were together again.

Rita had felt that the photographs she had seen in the papers were not of her husband, that she knew so well. He seemed so unlike himself—which was hardly surprising in view of the ordeal he had been through. Until this moment she had not been fully certain that her husband was alive. Even their telephone conversations had had an unreal quality. They were not enough to convince her.

But now, as she saw her husband lying in bed—good old Harry, just as he always was—she was finally able to relax a little and take joy in the moment. Harry had never shown the slightest sign of fear. Rita had never seen him nervous—except on their wedding day.

She realized her fear that Harry would be a changed man had been without foundation. He was as cheerful as ever.

"I'm finished with trawling," said Harry as he hugged and kissed his wife. Rita looked at him; she felt that he was saying this for her.

Deep down she knew that Harry would never be able to settle in an office, or in any job ashore. The man she had married, the man who was embracing her, was a seaman.

It was in his blood, simple as that.

"You'll never have to suffer anything like this again," said Harry. "I'll find a new living ashore."

Harry joked:

"I know taking a new job will make it impossible for us to pay off our house in three or four years as we hoped. Now I'll have to be a 25-year-mortgage man," he said.

Harry knew that if he left the sea his salary would drop drastically. He would say goodbye to the prospect of being captain of a ship, with nine or ten thousand pounds a year. If he went ashore he could hardly expect to earn more than twenty pounds a week—perhaps £1,200 to £1,400 a year.

"But I never want to go through this agony again. I could go on the buses or something like that," said Harry.

Everyone in the room smiled.

In spite of all he had been through, his only wish was to go back to sea. He knew he would be skipper of a ship within a few years. He had been at sea since the age of 15, and until this time it had never crossed his mind to find other work.

But he wanted to prevent his wife from any more sufferings in the future.

A hesitant knock was heard at the door. Harry's parents appeared in the doorway. The small hospital room was crowded.

Harry senior, a former seaman, greeted his son just as he did when he met him on the street in Hull:

"How are you, son?"

His son replied loud and clear that he was fine. His mother, Minnie, came over to her son, hugged him and said:

"It's good to see you, our Harry!"

The family kissed, hugged, and exchanged affectionate words.

A crowd eagerly awaits the arrival of Rita at the hospital in Isafjord.

❏ Bragi Guðmundsson

Medical director Dr. Ulfur Gunnarsson (wearing an overcoat, left of centre) speaks to reporters outside the hospital.

❏ Bragi Guðmundsson

Scuffles outside the hospital. Dr. Ulfur Gunnarsson tries to keep the press outside—all of them wanted to come inside to observe the reunion of the Eddoms.

❑ Ólafur K. Magnússon

After Rita had spent only ten minutes with her husband, it was decided that she would visit Harry again the following day. Rita felt her visit had been far too short. But the hospital doctors said that Harry must rest. Rita decided to not give Harry any more news of little Natalee until she saw him next.

When the photographer had taken his pictures, after having forced his way into the hospital along with a reporter, scuffles broke out again between him and the hospital staff. The Icelandic daily newspaper *Visir* reported that the photographer "would not do as he was asked until he had been well and truly thrashed."

Strange as it may seem, the *Sun* representatives had decided—although it was the middle of winter—to fly Rita down south to Reykjavik for the night, and then bring her back to

A Sun *reporter observes developments outside the hospital.*
❑ Bragi Guðmundsson

Isafjord the following day. This was intended to prevent other journalists making contact with Rita before their exclusive deal expired at midnight.

When Harry Eddom heard of the uproar, he assured all those he spoke to that he was sorry for the way matters had gone. On the Thursday evening Rita decided to take things easy at Hotel Saga in Reykjavik, have a drink and try to sleep. But she was still in a state of nervous tension and could not relax. Yet she felt she was the happiest woman in the world. She thought of what her husband had said:

"I'm finished with trawling."

Yet Rita knew that her husband would never be happy if he gave up the sea. He had been at sea since he was a youngster, and that was all he knew—it had never crossed his mind to do anything else. His father and his grandfather before him had been seamen. She knew that if Harry did as he said, it would be for her sake alone. She did not feel that would be right.

152

At the telephone company in Reykjavik, several women were busy sending journalists' photographs to Britain. When the *Sun's* journalist and photographer brought in the eagerly awaited exclusive photographs of Harry and Rita's kiss in the hospital room in Isafjord, telephonist Audur Proppé asked if they wanted to pop out for a bite to eat while the photographs were being sent down the line. Absolutely not. The *Sun* representatives said that the colleagues would do anything, "even murder," to get hold of those pictures.

As Harry thought of all his shipmates who had lost their lives, he remembered that Captain Philip Gay had asked him to help choose the crew for that fateful trip. And now all his shipmates were dead. "It's an awful responsibility to have to live with. But the sinking was no one's fault. We just took a sea. We were only two or three miles from the 3,000-foot walls of the fjord. We should have been safe as houses." And Harry thought especially of Wally Hewitt and Barry Rogers, who had hauled him unconscious into the life-raft, only to die themselves on the wild waves: "I shall never forget the two lads and how they died. They saved my life when they pulled me out of the sea."

Due to the media frenzy at the hospital, Dr. Ulfur Gunnarsson had had to postpone various surgical procedures that had been scheduled. And the patients in the hospital had witnessed the mob of reporters banging at doors and windows around them. A thirteen-year-old girl, Margret Oddsdottir, was in hospital in Isafjord. She had first heard the news of Harry Eddom on the little radio by her bed. She had also met him in the evenings, when peace settled over the hospital:

"He was a warm, handsome man. He gave me a nice smile when we met in the corridor. He was obviously a good man.

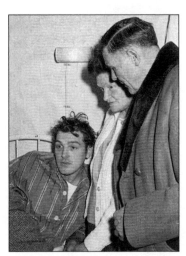

Harry with his parents—Harry senior and Minnie—at the hospital.
❏ Bragi Guðmundsson

Rita Eddom leaving the hospital at Isafjord.

❏ Bragi Guðmundsson

Over the past few days we kids had been very frightened—I knew some of the men who had sailed on the *Heidrun*. But it was wonderful that someone survived so miraculously in all that tragedy."

The loss of the *Heidrun* was a grave shock to the communities of Isafjord Bay. In a small village like Bolungarvik, where everybody knows everybody else, and many are also linked by family ties, the death of six men was a severe blow. The little community was all but paralyzed with grief.

Gudmundur Gudmundsson of the Life-Saving Association at Isafjord had not slept for the 48 hours of the storm, and had closely observed events:

"When Harry Eddom was found alive, I found it quite incredible that he could have survived—and after standing by the house wall for all those hours. Everyone was astonished. The only explanation could be that the man had an amazing constitution.

I see that as the most tragic event in the history of accidents at sea in Iceland—two ships being lost in Isafjord Bay, and another running aground, all at the same time.

But the crew of the *Notts County* owed their lives to the fact that the ship ran aground. Otherwise that trawler would have capsized like the others, and the crew would have perished.

It's easy to say, in retrospect, what's the right thing to do, but you'd never think anyone would deliberately run a ship aground. The skipper of the *Notts County* certainly didn't. Yet perhaps, in the state they were in, those other ships might have been saved if they had been sailed into shelter under Snæfjallaströnd, where the sea was shallow, and had lain at anchor there. But no doubt they couldn't have managed it in those conditions."

Physiologist Dr. Griffith Pugh, director of a medical research facility in London that made studies of stamina, travelled

155

The six-man crew of the Heidrun II: Left to right, upper row: Rögnvaldur Sigurjonsson, Pall Isleifur Vilhjalmsson and Kjartan Halldor Kjartansson. Left to right, lower row: Ragnar and Sigurjon Rögnvaldsson (sons of skipper Rögnvaldur) and Sigurdur Sigurdsson.

to Iceland to meet Harry Eddom, in order to seek some indication of how he had survived. Dr. Pugh had been on expeditions in the Himalayas with Sir Edmund Hillary, and to the South Pole with Sir Edmund and Vivian Fuchs.

Harry asked Dr. Pugh to explain why he should have survived. He said: "You simply had the will to live."

"But why me?" asked Harry.

"People's will to live is just variable. You can't explain it," he replied.

Physiologist Griffith Pugh examined Harry Eddom.

❑ Morgunblaðið

Harry had a lot to live for, he thought to himself—a loving wife, a baby, all his family. Yet he would continue to ask himself, why me? A question he could never answer.

Dr. Pugh said in an interview with Icelandic daily *Morgunblaðið* that there were two main factors that explained why Harry had survived:

"He was warmly dressed, in waterproof outer clothing, and he never lost hope. He kept his head."

After the storm, a life raft was washed up on the island of Vigur in Isafjord Bay. It turned out to be from the *Notts County*— it was the raft that had been launched first, which was caught by the wind and blown away like a kite.

The captain of the coastguard vessel *Odin*, Sigurdur Th. Arnason, found it incredible that someone had survived from the *Ross Cleveland*:

"I gave a lot of thought to why Harry Eddom had survived. It's unbelievable. Obviously, he must have been in excellent condition. But chance is an important factor too, under those circumstances. Luck was also on Harry's side. I thought it quite remarkable that he had been able to keep the life raft on an even keel all the way ashore in that storm. And he was lucky that the life raft was not damaged when it was launched from the sinking ship. Harry had no control over where the life raft was washed ashore. He saw a building, and at the point when he was completely exhausted and could do no more, someone found him. The dogs played a vital role. I'm not saying that Gudmann wouldn't have found Harry on his own. But it was really chance, in the events before Harry arrived on dry land, that made the difference between life and death."

When Harry had been in hospital in Isafjord for five days, yet more news was heard of British trawlermen in trouble off Iceland. The skipper of the *Blackburn Rovers* had been heading for Neskaupstadur on the east coast, but had mistakenly entered the next fjord, Mjoifjord, where the trawler collided with the dock and was damaged. The skipper then took his ship over to Neskaupstadur, but as she lay offshore there, she ran aground in shallows.

The ship was detained at Neskaupstadur for the incident to be investigated by a maritime court; after this, four of the crew of the *Blackburn Rovers* refused to sail with that skipper, especially in view of the recent losses off Iceland. Another British trawler, sailing for Iceland, had turned back when the crew refused to continue. Some went ashore when the ship docked on the Humber.

On February 15 a British meteorological observation vessel, the *Weather Reporter*, arrived in Iceland; the British government had sent her to provide guidance to British trawlers fishing off Iceland.

The survivors from the *Notts County* had been reunited with their loved ones. Dick Moore decided it was time for a change:

"When we got to Grimsby and the crew went to their homes, I decided I wouldn't sail on the trawlers any more. We were paid for that tour, and an additional bonus. But we never saw the things we had left on board the *Notts County* again—although the ship had been towed off the rocks.

I soon decided I would go to Norway to see my girlfriend I'd met in January. She had been a nurse in Honningsvaag at the north of Norway, but I'd heard that she had moved down south, to Drammen.

She was taken aback when I went to see her at the hospital there. Unfortunately, she wasn't very pleased to see me, as she'd met someone else—a Norwegian teacher in Drammen. But she gave me a friendly reception.

I was disappointed, of course. But I met some English people in Drammen, who worked in a paper mill. 'You ought to come and work with us,' one of them said, and so I got a job at the paper mill. I worked there for a while, and enjoyed it. Some time later a Norwegian ship arrived to collect a cargo of paper.

The crew was short one man!

I decided to take the berth. It was to be a fateful decision."

After eight days of excellent care at the hospital in Isafjord, Harry Eddom returned to the United Kingdom. The young couple were disappointed that they had not been able to thank young Gudmann of Kleifar and his parents for saving

Harry's life. It was not regarded as wise for Harry to travel by sea out to the isolated farmstead. But Harry and Gudmann would meet later.

Before Harry returned home, he received a gift of knitted gloves from an anonymous woman well-wisher in Akranes, west Iceland. She said he should make sure to wear the gloves the next time he was fishing off Iceland.

Harry sent her his sincere thanks.

On his arrival in England, he was given a hero's welcome. But this quiet, unassuming man chose to disappear quietly into his family life—for the time being at least.

Rita wanted to express her thanks to the lad at Kleifar. On March 26, 1968 she wrote:

> Dear Jon Gudmann
>
> I am very sorry this letter has been so late in reaching you, but we have had a bit of a misunderstanding in address, so may I now take the opportunity of thanking you for taking my husband Harry to your home, also your family for looking after him so well. If this had not been done, I am sure he would have died.
>
> I just don't know how to thank you all, as I know we will most probably never meet one another, but I shall never forget you, for you saved my husband's life.
>
> Please, I would like to send you something in return for what you all did, so would you write back and tell me how many family there is, and if there is anything you would like from England don't hesitate to ask, as I must send you something.

The City of Hull is still very sad at the great loss of so many brave fishermen who lost their lives, but with the help of God he will bring the families out of this ordeal.

I will tell you about Harry, he is very well indeed, he is out and about and has not had to have any toes taken off, but his toenails have started coming off. The Doctor says it is quite all right, he will grow them again.

He will most likely go back to sea but has not decided yet, so maybe one day you will meet him personally again and he will be able to thank you all again.

I will bring this letter to an end. I hope you will write to us. Thank you again, may God bless and keep you.

Yours sincerely,
Rita and Harry Eddom
Baby Natalee

Rita's prediction was to come true.

At around that time, Dick Moore was embarking in Norway:

"There were other Englishmen among the crew of the ship. I didn't know then what a mistake I was making. The ship—the *Devina*—was old. We sailed to England with a cargo of paper. After that we were to go all the way to Chicago in the USA, via Canada, with a cargo of iron ore.

On our journey across the Atlantic, we found ourselves in a bad storm. The ship pitched and rolled. The weight of the cargo was low down in the hold, so the ship bobbed around like a buoy.

An anonymous gift of knitted gloves from a woman in Akranes is presented to Harry Eddom by Geir Zoëga, agent for British shipping companies in Iceland.

❏ Kristinn Benediktsson

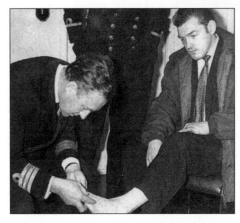

Captain J.F. Ryan examines Harry Eddom's feet for frostbite injury on his return to Hull.

❏ Dark Winter—The Hull Daily Mail

I realized it had been a mistake for me to go back to sea so soon after what had happened in Isafjord Bay. It had affected me more than I expected.

I was terrified, and desperate—I felt much as I did at the worst times in Iceland. At night I had nightmares, and in the end I couldn't sleep. I was always waking up, bathed in sweat and frightened, always checking whether the ship was going to sink.

I sometimes cried for hours at a time.

I was going to pieces. The skipper and first mate were very good to me, and did what they could to help me keep my head. They knew I had had a bad experience in Iceland in February—as news of it had spread all over Europe.

When we docked in Montreal, the Great Lakes workers were on strike, so we were delayed for some time. I didn't mind being on board ship, but I still had the nightmares.

As soon as I managed to fall asleep I would see Robert Bowie, my shipmate on the *Notts County*, over and over again, and hear his cries for help as he struggled in the life raft. Again and again, I lived through the storm and the icing, the howling gale, the hopeless efforts to save ourselves, the groaning of the grounded ship, the terror, and the fear of death.

I was in an appalling state. I was in such a state of nervous exhaustion after not sleeping for so long, that they decided to send me ashore in Canada to see a doctor. I asked him to give me something to help me sleep. "It would be best for you to go into hospital here in Montreal," said the doctor after talking to me.

I stayed in hospital for three weeks. The ship went on to Chicago, and I was sent home to England. But my troubles weren't over."

On May 2, 1968, it had been decided that the town of Grimsby would honour the crew of the coastguard vessel *Odin* for their bravery in rescuing eighteen local seamen. Three months had passed since the events in Isafjord Bay.

Captain Sigurdur Th. Arnason, first mate Sigurjon Hannesson and second mate Palmi Hlödversson were to go to England.

Sigurjon Hannesson recalls the journey:

"It was a very enjoyable trip. We were given a wonderful reception in England. Pall Heidar Jonsson, who worked for Icelandair, acted as our guide. We rented a car in London and drove north to Grimsby.

Rita and little Natalee Eddom wait for Dad to come home. Harry flew to Glasgow, and was driven home to Hull under police escort.

❏ Dark Winter—The Hull Daily Mail

In Grimsby we were invited to a meeting of the town council, where the councillors were wearing wigs and all that. I remember that a photographer had been brought in to take pictures of the ceremony.

Then the ceremony was held, very solemn and formal. When it was over, the mayor turned to the photographer and asked: 'Have you got all the pictures you want?'

The photographer replied, rather embarrassed, 'I haven't taken any yet!'

'Well, why not?' asked the mayor.

'I didn't like to interrupt the ceremony. I thought it was so impressive,' the man replied.

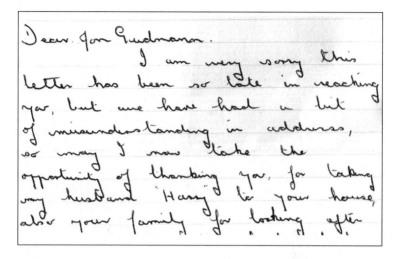

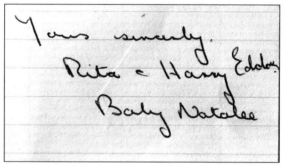

Rita Eddom's letter of thanks to Gudmann Gudmundsson.

But the mayor was quick to put things right. 'That's all right. We'll just act it all over again and you can take pictures,' he said. They did so, and the photographer got the pictures he needed.

So the whole ceremony was actually carried out twice."

Captain Sigurdur Arnason was also impressed by the ceremony. He had the opportunity to meet once again a man, in his

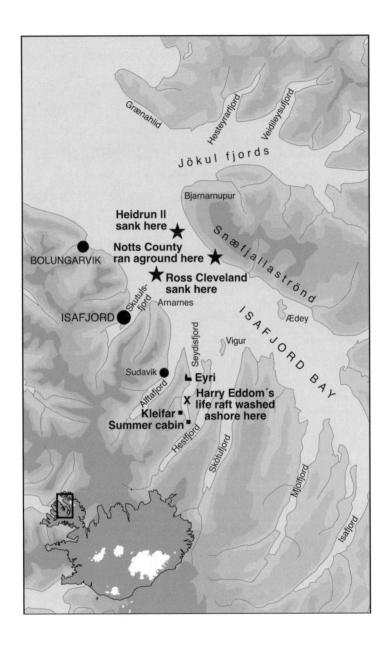

early forties, who had been in a state of emotional turmoil when the crew of the *Notts County* were rescued. When the two men had met briefly on the bridge of the *Odin*, he had been on the brink of nervous collapse, and had declared that he would never go to sea again.

Today he was quite different. The man, who all agreed had shown remarkable courage and determination in keeping up the spirits of his crew during their hard night and morning in the grounded trawler, had made a good recovery. He had lost a finger to frostbite, but now he was sailing on another trawler from the Humber. Sigurdur was pleased to see Captain George Burres again:

"The captain of the *Notts County* urged me to join him at a place in Grimsby where the skippers met up. But unfortunately I had a prior engagement, to visit an Icelandic woman who lived locally, after the council meeting. I couldn't let her down, but I would have liked to join him.

I enjoyed talking to George Burres. He was a very intelligent man."

At about that time Harry Eddom had made a decision which had been much discussed and thought about in his family since the *Ross Cleveland* went down—ought he to go back to sea? His conclusion was that he would do so, at least for the time being, to see how it went. In the spring he sailed as first mate on the trawler *Stella Carina* from Hull, and later on the *Ross Illustrious*. Harry was determined not to allow himself to be defeated by what had happened in Isafjord Bay. He had decided he would do his best to forget.

At the end of October Harry attended a maritime court in his home town, Hull. Hannes Hafstein of the Icelandic Life-Saving Association and meteorologist Hlynur Sigtryggsson travelled to England to give testimony on various matters regarding Iceland,

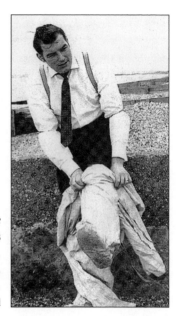

Harry Eddom with the duck suit he was wearing when the Ross Cleveland *foundered. He had paid £7 for the suit, which was to save his life.*
❏ Dark Winter—The Hull Daily Mail

at the request of the British investigators. They were also to testify with reference to the disappearance of the *Kingston Peridot*. Hannes Hafstein's evidence demonstrated that the *Kingston Peridot* had not run aground, but been lost at sea, and this meant that the crew's widows were eligible for much higher compensation. The vessel operators had maintained that the ship had run aground—hence that the principal cause had been human error. But Hannes's testimony led to the court reaching the conclusion that the ship had been lost out at sea, and that she could hardly have been deemed seaworthy—at least for fishing off Iceland.

It was noticeable at the court proceedings that, although almost nine months had passed since the events in Isafjord Bay, the

Support ship Orsino *sails out of the Humber through the locks. Her role was to monitor weather forecasts and assist British trawlers off Iceland. The campaign of Lil Bilocca and the other trawlermen's wives had yielded results.*

❏ Dark Winter—The Hull Daily Mail

seamen who gave testimony, many of whom had been aboard the *Notts County,* had great difficulty in speaking of the experience. In a book about the rescue, Hannes Hafstein explained that many of the crew had been deeply traumatized—they had abandoned all hope, and simply passively awaited their fate. As the men described the weather, and their experiences that night, it was clear

George Burres, skipper of the Notts County, *with coastguards Captain Sigurdur Th. Arnason, second mate Palmi Hlödversson and first mate Sigurjon Hannesson of the* Odin, *at a meeting of Grimsby Town Council in May 1968*

Coastguards are presented with a plaque from Grimsby Town Council honouring them for the rescue. The plaque now hangs aboard the Odin.

Hannes Hafstein (left) of the Icelandic Life-Saving Association with Harry Eddom at maritime court in Hull, October 1968.

❑ The Hull Daily Mail

Tests of a life raft from the Kingston Peridot, *found in north Iceland. There was no sign that anyone had escaped from the sinking ship into the life raft. Hannes Hafstein of the Icelandic Life-Saving Association, left.*

❏ Bragi Guðmundsson

that they were going through the horrors again, and some were so overcome by emotion that they could hardly speak.

That summer, Dick Moore was still suffering the psychological after-effects of his ordeal off Iceland:

"For a while I went from job to job. But I couldn't get rid of the nightmares, and eventually I finished up in a psychiatric unit in England for five weeks.

Later that year I got work at Dover on a ship laying telephone cables and sailed between the Scottish isles. By this time, I didn't feel uncomfortable at sea. Just before Christmas, the ship docked in Clydebank near Glasgow. The whole crew went ashore, to a pub called the Seven Seas on the Kilbowie Road.

To cut a long story short, a beautiful, kind young lady was working in the pub, who got talking to me. We had a long conversation. I wanted to ask her out for a meal. She told me to wait for

Ceremony aboard the Odin *when British ambassador Halford Macleod presented Captain Sigurdur Arnason with an OBE, and the first and second mate with the Sea Gallantry Medal. Left to right: Sigurdur Arnason with his wife Edda Jonsdottir, Sigurjon Hannesson with his wife Maggy Björg Jonsdottir, and Palmi Hlödversson with his wife Gudmunda Helgadottir.*

❏ Morgunblaðið

her at the back door. I did so, she sneaked out, and we had a good evening together.

Eight months later, on August 13, 1969, we were married.

That was Elizabeth—who is my wife today. We live in a suburb of Glasgow, and we have three children and four grandchildren. I've been happy and had a good life after I met my wife, and got over the experience I had. But it's undeniable that it took me a long time to recover.

The crew of the Odin, *April 28, 1968.*
Front row, left to right: radio operator Valdimar Jonsson, third mate
Sigurjon Ingi Sigurjonsson, second mate Palmi Hlödversson, first mate
Sigurjon Hannesson, captain Sigurdur Th. Arnason, first engineer Larus
Magnusson, second engineer Georg Jonsson, third engineer Haraldur
Johannsson and fourth engineer Ragnar Steinsson.
Back row, left to right: mess boys Gudmundur Petursson, Sigurdur
Johannsson and Gudmundur E. Björnsson, deckhands Torfi Geirmundsson,
Tryggvi Bjarnason and Haukur Jonsson (galley hand), deckhand Birgir
Oskarsson, deckhand Gudmundur Kjartansson, boatswain Egill Palsson,
deckhand Olafur Th. Ragnarsson, deckhand Valgardur Magnusson, oiler
Alfred Larusson, oiler Agnar Einarsson, deckhand Petur Ludviksson, and
Björn H. Björnsson (engine room). At the front is the ship's dog, Freyja.
Three members of the crew, second engineer Bjarni Gudbjörnsson, deckhand
Birgir Th. Jonsson and Larus Eggertsson (engine room), are absent. The
photograph was taken by galley hand Adolf Hansen.

Dick Moore and his wife Elizabeth on their wedding day, August 13, 1968, at St. Stephen's Church, Clydebank.

I think the main reason for my feeling so bad was that I felt guilty about the lad who died on the *Notts County*. I kept hearing him calling out: 'Help me, help me!' It haunted me dreadfully. But his death wasn't anybody's fault. We couldn't get him aboard—there was no way—until it was too late.

Never in my life have I been as terrified as I was in that appalling storm. You're never the same again when you've looked death in the face as we did on board that ship."

At the end of 1968, Rita gave birth to a son, Jason. Harry earned his skipper's ticket in 1969, and became a captain of trawlers sailing from Hull—until 1972, when the Icelanders extended their fishing limits to 50 miles, leading to the "Cod Wars," in which British ships continued to fish off Iceland, under the protection of the Royal Navy, while the Iceland Coastguard, with its small gunboats, did its best to keep them out. Feelings ran so high that Iceland and the UK called home their ambassadors in each other's capitals, and the British embassy in Reykjavik was pelted with rocks by protesters.

Harry Eddom was to clash with the Iceland Coastguard many times during his years as a trawler skipper. When the author asked him about those times during the Cod Wars, he simply replied:

"Each of us was simply doing what he had to do."

In December 1970, a little less than two years after Harry Eddom's rescue, Gudmann Gudmundsson of Kleifar was a member of the crew of the *Gudrun*, a fishing boat from Hafnarfjord, which sailed to England to sell her catch. Journalists in Grimsby got wind of the fact that the lad who had saved Harry Eddom's life was in town. The following news item was published:

Greetings to a young lifesaver

A grateful trawler wife sent a Christmas greeting telegram to a young Icelandic fisherman in Grimsby yesterday.

It was a very special telegram. For two-and-a-half years ago, he saved the life of her husband— Harry Eddom, the sole survivor of the Hull trawler *Ross Cleveland*.

When the trawler sank in a gale off Iceland's north-west coast, Mr. Eddom managed to scramble into a life raft and make for the shore.

He staggered, exhausted and suffering from frostbite, up the beach to an old outhouse. There he was found by Gudmann Gudmundsson, then a 14-year-old shepherd lad.

Gudmann, now a deckhand on the trawler Gudrun, managed to carry him back to the farmhouse half a mile away where his mother gave him warm clothing and food.

He planned to visit Mrs. Eddom at her home in Hull yesterday, but had to cancel the trip because his ship was sailing early.

He recalled: "I don't know how I got him back to the farm. He was very weak and very heavy. I think he would have died if he had stayed out in the cold much longer.

"I would have liked to see Mrs. Eddom. But because of the time, I cannot get over. I would like to send the whole family my best wishes for Christmas.

And the next time I come to Grimsby I shall do my best to visit them."

When Mrs. Eddom heard Gudmann was in Britain, she immediately contacted the Post Office and sent a greetings telegram to the ship.

She said she was disappointed he could not come across the Humber.

Gudmann was nearly twenty, and was working in Isafjord, when Harry Eddom revisited the town:

"I met Harry some years after the events on Isafjord Bay. I was nineteen then. I was working at sea, and living in Isafjord. Harry was on a British trawler which had come in to Isafjord. A cousin of mine came to see me. Harry had been asking after me, and wanted me to come and meet him. He was at Doctor Ulfur's home, and he'd heard I was in town too. He and the doctor were having a pleasant reunion.

I went over to Ulfur's house, and Harry and I met again. I still didn't speak any English, but my cousin who came with me

Gudmann Gudmundsson — "See you next time."

Greetings to young lifesaver

The Grimsby Telegraph reported on young Gudmann Gudmundsson's visit to Hull.

interpreted for us. Harry and I remembered each other well, of course. After we'd been at Ulfur's for a while, Harry took us back to his ship, and had a good meal cooked for us. Then we shared some drinks, and sat far into the night.

We got along well—Harry's a fine man. He was very grateful to me."

When reporters finally managed to make the trip over to Kleifar in February 1968 to interview Gudmann after he rescued Harry Eddom, the young lad said he planned to go to sea. He was asked whether the horrifying events on Isafjord Bay would

Gudmann Gudmundsson (right) with the author in Seydisfjord, outside the abandoned farmhouse at Kleifar. In the middle of the photograph, just beyond where Gudmann is pointing, is the small summer cabin where Harry Eddom spent a freezing night hoping to be rescued.

❏ Gunnar V. Andrésson

Gudmann points out Lækir on the opposite shore of the fjord, where the life raft was washed ashore. Harry Eddom walked from there to the head of the fjord, about three kilometres over rough territory, much of it in the dark.

❏ Gunnar V. Andrésson

The leeward side of the cabin, where Harry Eddom took shelter. Gudmann stands where he found the shipwrecked man.

❏ Gunnar V. Andrésson

discourage him from this plan, he answered firmly "no." He was determined to accept whatever happened to him.

"I was to experience danger at sea myself later. In 1989 I was alone on a small shrimper, the *Gudmundur Asgeirsson*—she was a small nine-tonner that took the trawl in at the stern. The winch was aft. I'd put the boat in forward gear, and released the fishing gear, but I was just a bit too quick. I stepped into the sweepline, which caught around my leg and whipped me overboard.

The boat sailed on, towing me behind.

As I was pulled along behind the boat, I managed to get hold of the ladder at the stern. I made sure not to let go, and then tried to slip my boot off. But it was difficult—the cable tightened around my leg, pulled taut between the boat and the trawl.

180

Inside the now-deserted farmhouse at Kleifar. In this kitchen, in the warmth of an oil-fired stove, Harry Eddom finally relaxed and slept after his 36-hour ordeal.

❑ Gunnar V. Andrésson

I thought my time was up.

It took quite a long time for me to free myself. With difficulty I got back on board, and then rested for a long time on the deck. I'd had an awful shock. But then I went on fishing for the rest of the day. As I hung behind the boat I thought about my family—my wife Ragnheidur and our three children.

For a long time I told no one what had happened, not even Ragnheidur. She didn't find out until months later, when she was looking for a woolly sock that I'd lost with the boot. I found I had to confess what had happened.

A few years later a wooden boat capsized under me out in Isafjord Bay. That time I managed to send a Mayday call and get into a life raft. A rescue team came out and found me.

Even later, I co-owned a thirty-ton boat, *Dröfn*, with another man. We were fishing for shrimp in Hestfjord. On our way home we hit bad weather and a nasty swell. The boat's engine broke down just off Tjaldtangi, and we were drifting fast onto the skerry. One wave carried the boat up onto the skerry and the bulwarks were torn off. The next wave swept her off, and the third carried us right up onto the shore. It all went well in the end."

Gudmann has often thought about Harry walking along the fjord that night:

"It must have taken Harry a long time to get to the summer cabin—it's about three kilometres over rough terrain. And he went a far more difficult route than we use. His tracks were mostly close to the shoreline. But he had to climb up over rocks where there are vertical cliffs at the shore. When he got beyond Kleifahvammur there was a difficult section of rocky ground before he reached the head of the fjord.

He must have been walking at dusk and then in pitch darkness. He couldn't see any light from our house. We didn't have electricity, and there were no outside lights. There were only oil lamps in the windows that faced inland, so he could hardly have noticed them.

Harry may have reached the cabin by about midnight on the Monday night. And he stood there by the wall for at least ten hours—all night long and into the morning.

I think that another contributing factor in Harry's survival was that the wind dropped and the temperature rose on the Monday night."

Sigurjon Hannesson, who now works for the Port of Reykjavik, looks back on seamanship in the sixties and seventies as a memorable, historic period, when Britons and Icelanders clashed in various ways.

"At that time we would hear that in England they sometimes had to go into the pubs to man the ships. It was similar to the way things used to be in Iceland in the heyday of the herring fishery. In those days the trawlers would lie at anchor in the outer harbour while someone went into town to find more men to crew the vessel.

I was taken aback when I saw those men file out of the wheelhouse waving bottles of booze. They could have endangered all of us, and you couldn't tell what they might do. If one of them had had the idea of jumping overboard to us, and been followed by others, I don't know how it would have ended. The atmosphere also seemed very odd—the men had thrown all their life rafts overboard. But nobody appeared to be inebriated.

I must say, I wouldn't have minded having a film of myself, when I stood in the rescue boat, encrusted with ice from head to toe, shook my fist at them and gave them a talking-to."

Palmi Hlödversson, who now teaches at the Seamen's College in Reykjavik, still recalls those days in early February 1968 with great clarity:

"The worst thing I experienced during those few days was climbing the mast to knock the ice off the radar scanner. That was really far more risky than the actual rescue of the crew off the grounded trawler. You really needed both hands to get the ice off. You could have done with a third hand, and even a fourth, to hold on with. I hung by a rope—and the mast, which was normally about fifteen centimetres in diameter, was covered in such a thick coating of ice that I couldn't even reach around it."

Captain Sigurdur Th. Arnason is now retired, living in Reykjavik.

"The happiness of being able to help our fellow-men and save their lives is fresh in my mind—but I also think of our sorrow at not being able to save the lives of the men on the *Heidrun II*. The

Captain Sigurdur Th. Arnason.

❑ Brynjar Gauti Sveinsson

period after the rescue was very hard for me. I must admit that when people wrote in the papers, making all sorts of allegations about what we'd done, I didn't like it at all. People were keen to lay blame, but they were the ones who had no idea what they were talking about." Allegations were made that the coastguards might have saved the Icelanders aboard the *Heidrun*, but gave priority to the British vessels.

"When you have an experience like that, everyone tries to do his duty, and help his fellow-men, if he can.

It's true, that over all these years I've mulled it over.

Maybe I was wrong in not talking it over with my shipmates, like Sigurjon and Palmi. But I suppressed it, kept my mouth shut,

Radio operator
Valdimar Jonsson.
❑ Brynjar Gauti Sveinsson

and tried to get over it on my own. But every seaman knows that the safety of your own ship has to come first. We were struggling with icing, like the other vessels, and we had take shelter. We had no hope of helping anyone, until the worst of the storm had started to abate. I would have been letting my own men down if I hadn't made that my first priority."

Radio operator Valdimar Jonsson now lives in Mosfellsbær adjacent to Reykjavik. He is the son-in-law of Gudmundur Gudmundsson, who co-ordinated rescue operations from Isafjord:

"My father-in-law has often remarked: 'Who would ever have thought that a six- or seven-hundred-ton ship could go down here—two or three miles off Arnarnes? No one at all.'

185

Gudmundur Gudmundsson.

The ships should have been safe in shelter there.

We learned that the crew of the *Ross Cleveland* had been reluctant to go out on deck to clear the ice off. Before she went down, there were only three or four men at a time out on deck chopping at the ice. And you can't help wondering why the *Ross Cleveland* capsized, but not the other trawlers. Probably the others had had more success in clearing the ice off, and fighting for their lives."

Gudmundur Gudmundsson is now 85 years old, living in Isafjord:

"It was a remarkable event, in that there was nothing that could be done to help anyone for a time. I was born and brought

Torfi Geirmundsson.
❑ Brynjar Gauti Sveinsson

up here on Isafjord Bay, I'd been a skipper for more than twenty years, and experienced all sorts of weathers and dangerous conditions. But it was obvious that the men simply couldn't manage to keep the ice at bay. I'd been in conditions like that myself. It would happen when we'd been fishing off Isafjord Bay, and were sailing home into the wind in sub-zero temperatures. Then we always had to run tail to wind while we cleared the ice off. You could always tell from the vessel's movements where the centre of gravity was, and you had to take action.

That's the probable explanation for the loss of the *Heidrun II* and the *Ross Cleveland*. Both ships capsized due to the build-up of ice. And the crew of the *Notts County* had the same problem.

*Second mate Palmi
Hlödversson*
❏ Brynjar Gauti Sveinsson

But in their case, they were fortunate enough to run aground before she turned over.

Before that, I would never have thought that could ever happen—that amount of icing inside Isafjord Bay. But the gale was so strong, and sea was always washing over the ships—and the frost was bitter."

Harry Eddom has become the subject of poetry and songs—in his home town he became something of a living legend. But he continued to go to sea.

In 1981 Harry lost his wife Rita, at the age of only 42, of a viral infection. Harry felt the loss of Rita bitterly. Soon after her death he was sent to the Persian Gulf as captain of supply ships.

*First mate Sigurjon
Hannesson.*
❏ Brynjar Gauti Sveinsson

Harry is away for long periods, up to three months at a time. He then returns to Hull for three to six weeks at a time. His daughter, Natalee, now 34, teaches hairdressing in a Hull secondary school. Her brother Jason, a little over a year younger, has had various different jobs, including diving. Today Harry Eddom is sixty years old. He lives in Cottingham with a new partner:

"When my wife died the fisheries in England were dying, at least in their old form. So I turned to new work. But I have no complaints. I'm doing all right—I can afford to pay my bills, at least.

I was told that the storm in Isafjord Bay was the worst for forty years—or since 1925. I don't doubt it."

Agust Gardarsson, one of the party who went into Seydisfjord in search of survivors.
❏ Halldór Sveinbjörnsson

* * *

Dick Moore now lives in Old Kilpatrick, a suburb of Glasgow:

"Now, 33 years after the events on Isafjord Bay, I've spoken to people in Grimsby. A journalist there mentioned reports which said that the man who died on the *Notts County* had jumped down into the life raft in panic.

That's not right, in my view.

Robert Bowie did what he thought was right in the circumstances. We were told to launch the life raft. He showed initiative and courage when he jumped overboard to try and keep the raft steady on the water, so that the others could get down more easily. If he hadn't jumped overboard, and if the boat had tipped up,

Jon Ragnarsson, one of those who brought Harry Eddom from Seydisfjord to Isafjord.

❑ Halldór Sveinbjörnsson

it's quite likely that others would have tried to abandon ship. We saw that would be fatal. So you could say he saved other men from sharing his fate.

I remember at the maritime court, that Robert was said to have been taken below after the boat was washed aboard. But I maintain that never happened. Robert was inside the life raft when we left it on the deck and went up onto the bridge. He didn't die in a cabin as someone said. He was already dead when the life raft was washed aboard."

When Dick Moore lay in his cold, damp, uncomfortable room in Cleethorpes at the end of January 1968, and was called

The Moores at home in Old Kilpatrick outside Glasgow.

Dick Moore (right) with his eldest son, Anthony.

out to join the *Notts County*, he was a young man, who had few worldly possessions to his name. His sea bag was big enough to contain all he owned. He was to lose it all, but in return he received the biggest gift of all—his life.

Dick looks back after 33 years:

"Admittedly I lost everything—the only thing I took with me was my Parker pen, and I gave that away. But my family pictures, including pictures of my late mother, were lost with the *Notts County*. I heard that the ship had later been towed into port, but I never saw any of my possessions again.

It was a long night—the longest of my life. The night I prayed, and found a faith I hadn't known was in me.

I wouldn't hesitate to say that I thank Sigurdur Arnason, captain of the *Odin*, and all his crew for my life—and for the fact that I met my wife, and we had our three children. Many of the men already had children, who would have been fatherless if we had not survived.

I have strong feelings of gratitude to the Icelanders. During the Cod Wars, I always hated to hear that British naval vessels were ramming Iceland Coastguard vessels, especially in the case of the *Odin*."

In late 2001, Dick Moore decided to visit Iceland with his wife, Elizabeth. He wanted to take this opportunity to thank the crew of the *Odin* for saving his life, and show his wife—whom he met that same year as the events took place in Isafjord Bay—the northern land he had so often spoken of to her, and to their children and grandchildren: the family who might not be alive today, he says, were it not for the courage and bravery of the crew of the rescue ship *Odin*, that night.

Harry Eddom too decided to visit Iceland again, with his daughter Natalee, who was seven months old when her mother,

193

Harry Eddom in Hull. Harry, now in his sixties, is still sailing, now in the Persian Gulf as a skipper of supply ships for oil rigs.

Rita, went to see Harry in Iceland in 1968. They were not able to make the planned trip, as Harry was called out to the Persian Gulf. But Harry and Natalee plan to make a visit later, and meet Gudmann Gudmundsson and his family when the opportunity arises.

The last words belong to Harry:

"The Icelanders have been like brothers to me. God bless them all."

Afterword

On November 23, 2001, when the original Icelandic version of "Doom in the Deep" was published, a reception was arranged where the men who rescued Dick Moore welcomed him at a ceremony on board the *Odin*. Dick presented Sigurdur, Palmi, Sigurjon and Valdimar with silver-plated engraved bottles from Scotland as a token of gratitude to them for saving his life.

When the men had been given these gifts, Palmi stepped forward, looked Dick firmly in the eye and took out a beautiful Icelandic beach stone, with a silver plaque on it inscribed with the words: "From the crew of the *Odin*." All present, including a large contingent of reporters, watched with interest when Palmi said:

"Here you are, Richard, I hope you remember us."

On top of the stone was a holder. And what was resting on it? Yes—a silver-plated Parker pen, Dick's heirloom from all those years ago.

An emotional reunion culminates in happiness that will last forever. Dick Moore is presented with the silver-plated Parker pen he carried through hours of peril on the Notts County, *now returned to him on a stand of Icelandic rock with a silver plaque, a gift from those who saved his life. Left to right: first mate Sigurjon Hannesson, radio operator Valdimar Jonsson, Captain Sigurdur Th. Arnason, Dick Moore.*

Dick was lost for words at this unexpected and incredibly thoughtful gesture. He was moved, his eyes filled with tears—he thought of all his mates from the *Notts County* who were unable to attend this remarkable ceremony. In spite of the Cod War, strong bonds of friendship had been sealed even more firmly as these two nations commemorated their shared battle with the elements of the North Atlantic, which cost both sides the lives of so many brave "sons" who perished at sea.